NO ONE HAS TO DIE IN

John R.

Table of Contents

Introduction

Key Takeaways

Brief overview of substance abuse among seniors

Importance of addressing the unique challenges faced by senior citizens.

Purpose of the book: providing a comprehensive guide to recovery for seniors

Frequently Asked Questions

Conclusion

Chapter 1: Understanding Substance Abuse in Seniors

Key Takeaways

Prevalence of Substance Abuse in Seniors

Risk Factors for Substance Abuse in Aging Adults

Common Substances Abused by Seniors

Physical and Mental Health Implications of Substance Abuse in Seniors

Social Isolation and Substance Abuse in Older Adults

Recognizing the Signs of Substance Abuse in Aging Individuals

Strategies for Prevention and Intervention in Senior Substance Abuse

Frequently Asked Questions

Conclusion

Chapter 2: Recognizing the Signs of Substance Abuse and Seeking Help

Key Takeaways

Common Signs of Substance Abuse in Seniors

Physical Indicators of Substance Abuse in Older Adults

Behavioral Changes Associated with Substance Abuse in Seniors

Emotional and Psychological Symptoms of Substance Abuse in Older Individuals

Steps to Take in Seeking Help for Seniors Struggling with Substance Abuse

Frequently Asked Questions

Conclusion

Chapter 3: Creating a Supportive Environment

Key Takeaways

Understanding the Unique Needs of Seniors

Creating a Safe and Secure Physical Environment

Fostering Emotional Support and Connection

Providing Accessible and Age-Appropriate Treatment Options

Promoting Holistic Healing and Wellness

Frequently Asked Questions

Conclusion

Chapter 4: Tailored Treatment Approaches

Key Takeaways

Factors Contributing to Senior Substance Abuse

Specialized Treatment Strategies for Seniors

Addressing Unique Challenges of Aging Population

Creating an Environment for Senior Recovery

Importance of Sensitivity in Senior Substance Abuse Treatment

Frequently Asked Questions

Conclusion

Chapter 5: Developing Healthy Coping Mechanisms

Key Takeaways

Understanding the Impact of Substance Abuse on Seniors

Identifying Unhealthy Coping Mechanisms in Seniors

Promoting Self-Care and Emotional Well-being

Encouraging Supportive Relationships and Community Involvement

Implementing Effective Treatment and Recovery Strategies

Frequently Asked Questions

Conclusion

Chapter 6: Addressing Co-Occurring Health Issues

Key Takeaways

Growing Prevalence of Senior Substance Abuse

Understanding Co-Occurring Health Issues

Impact of Substance Abuse on Physical Health

Mental Health Challenges and Substance Abuse

Effective Interventions for Seniors' Recovery

Frequently Asked Questions

Conclusion

Chapter 7: Relapse Prevention Strategies

Key Takeaways

Understanding the Unique Challenges for Seniors

Identifying Triggers and High-Risk Situations

Building a Strong Support System

Developing Coping Mechanisms and Stress Management Techniques

Creating a Healthy and Structured Daily Routine

Frequently Asked Questions

Conclusion

Chapter 8: Rebuilding Relationships and Community Ties

Key Takeaways

Understanding the Impact of Substance Abuse on Relationships

Identifying Barriers to Rebuilding Community Ties

Strategies for Rebuilding Trust with Loved Ones

Reconnecting With Supportive Community Resources

Maintaining Healthy Relationships in Recovery

Frequently Asked Questions

Conclusion

Chapter 9: Navigating Legal and Financial Challenges

Key Takeaways

Understanding the Legal Implications

Identifying Financial Resources

Advocating for Legal Rights

Overcoming Financial Barriers

Navigating Legal and Financial Support Systems

Frequently Asked Questions

Conclusion

Conclusion:

The Power of Supportive Relationships

Embracing Self-Care and Wellness

Celebrating Victories, Big and Small

INTRODUCTION

As our population continues to age, it is crucial that we address the often-overlooked issue of substance abuse among seniors. While substance abuse may not be the first thing that comes to mind when we think of this demographic, the reality is that it is a growing problem with serious consequences.

In this book, we will explore the unique challenges faced by seniors, the risk factors that contribute to substance abuse in this population, and the impact it has on their health. Additionally, we will investigate the importance of addressing these challenges and providing recovery resources specifically tailored for seniors.

Prepare to be enlightened as we uncover the hidden world of substance abuse in seniors and discover the path towards recovery.

Key Takeaways

- Substance abuse among seniors is a growing problem with serious consequences.
- Seniors may face unique challenges such as retirement, loss of loved ones, chronic pain, and loneliness, which contribute to substance abuse.
- Healthcare professionals, caregivers, and family members should be educated about the signs, risks, and available resources to help seniors overcome substance abuse.
- Substance abuse among seniors can have a significant impact on their physical and mental

health, exacerbating existing conditions and weakening the immune system.

Brief overview of substance abuse among seniors

As individuals age, they may face unique challenges that can increase their vulnerability to substance abuse. It is important to have a brief overview of substance abuse among seniors to better understand this growing issue.

This overview will explore the factors that contribute to substance abuse among seniors, the risk factors they face, and the impact it can have on their health.

Growing Senior Substance Abuse

Substance abuse among seniors is a growing concern that requires compassionate and knowledgeable attention. As the population ages, there is an increasing number of older adults struggling with substance misuse. This issue is often overlooked, but it is essential to address it proactively.

There are several factors contributing to the rise in senior substance abuse. Retirement, loss of loved ones, chronic pain, and loneliness are just a few examples. Seniors may turn to alcohol, prescription drugs, or illicit substances to cope with these challenges.

It is crucial to approach this issue with empathy and understanding. Healthcare professionals, caregivers, and family members should be educated about the signs, risks, and available resources to help seniors overcome substance abuse. By providing support and assistance, we can ensure the well-being and dignity of our aging population.

Risk Factors for Seniors

Seniors face unique challenges that can contribute to substance abuse, making it crucial to understand the risk factors involved.

As individuals age, they often experience significant life changes such as retirement, loss of loved ones, declining health, and increased social isolation. These factors can lead to feelings of loneliness, boredom, and depression, which may increase the likelihood of turning to substances as a coping mechanism.

Additionally, seniors may have easier access to prescription medications, which can be misused or abused. Age-related changes in metabolism and physical health can also increase the vulnerability of seniors to the negative effects of substances.

Understanding these risk factors is essential to develop effective prevention and intervention strategies, and to provide the support and resources necessary to address substance abuse among seniors in a compassionate and informed manner.

Impact on Health

With advancing age, individuals may face significant health implications because of substance abuse. Substance abuse among seniors can lead to a wide range of physical and mental health problems.

Older adults are more susceptible to the adverse effects of substance abuse due to age-related changes in their bodies and increased vulnerability. Chronic substance abuse can weaken the immune system, making seniors more prone to infections and diseases. Additionally, substance abuse can exacerbate existing health conditions such as cardiovascular disease, diabetes, and respiratory problems.

Mental health issues such as depression, anxiety, and cognitive decline can also arise because of substance abuse. It is crucial to address substance abuse in seniors promptly to prevent further deterioration of their health and overall well-being.

Importance of addressing the unique challenges faced by senior citizens.

Addressing the unique challenges faced by senior citizens in relation to substance abuse is of utmost importance.

Aging-related risk factors such as chronic pain and cognitive decline can increase vulnerability to substance abuse.

Social isolation and loneliness, which are prevalent among seniors, can also contribute to the development or exacerbation of substance abuse issues.

Additionally, comorbid health conditions can complicate treatment and require a comprehensive approach to address both the substance abuse and the underlying medical issues.

Aging-Related Risk Factors

As individuals age, they encounter a multitude of unique challenges that require careful consideration and understanding. Aging-related risk factors play a significant role in the development of substance abuse issues among seniors. These factors include physical health decline, chronic pain, mental health disorders, social isolation, and the loss of loved ones.

Physical health decline can lead to the use of prescription medications, which can be misused or abused. Chronic pain can drive seniors to seek relief through self-medication with substances such as alcohol or opioids. Mental health disorders, such as depression and anxiety, can increase the risk of substance abuse as seniors may turn to drugs or alcohol as a coping mechanism.

Social isolation and the loss of loved ones can also contribute to feelings of loneliness and sadness, leading seniors to turn to substances for solace. Understanding and addressing these aging-related risk factors is essential in providing effective intervention and prevention strategies for substance abuse in seniors.

Social Isolation and Loneliness

Seniors face unique challenges in their later years, and one of the most pressing issues that needs to be addressed is the social isolation and loneliness they often experience.

As individuals age, they may lose loved ones, retire, or experience physical limitations that can limit their social interactions. These factors, combined with societal attitudes that dismiss the importance of social connections in old age, can lead to a sense of isolation and loneliness among seniors.

It is crucial to recognize the impact of social isolation and loneliness on the mental and physical well-being of older adults. Research has shown that seniors who feel socially isolated are at a higher risk of developing substance abuse issues.

Therefore, it is essential to prioritize interventions that promote social engagement, connection, and support for our aging population, ensuring they receive the care and attention they deserve.

Comorbid Health Conditions

With the unique challenges faced by senior citizens, it is imperative to recognize and address the comorbid health conditions that often accompany aging. Seniors are more likely to have multiple chronic health conditions, such as heart disease, diabetes, arthritis, and respiratory problems. These conditions can significantly impact their physical and mental well-being, making them more vulnerable to substance abuse.

Chronic pain, for example, can lead to the misuse of prescription pain medications. Additionally, the presence of comorbid conditions can complicate the treatment of substance abuse in seniors, requiring a comprehensive and individualized approach. Healthcare providers must consider the interactions between medications, potential side effects, and the overall health status of seniors when developing treatment plans.

Purpose of the book: providing a comprehensive guide to recovery for seniors

As the number of seniors struggling with substance abuse continues to rise, it is crucial to provide them with the necessary tools and resources for recovery.

This book aims to fill the gap in knowledge and support for this often-overlooked demographic group.

Unique Challenges for Seniors

Navigating the path to recovery later in life presents a distinct set of challenges for individuals seeking to overcome substance abuse. Seniors face unique obstacles as they embark on their journey to sobriety.

Firstly, there is often a lack of awareness and recognition of substance abuse among older adults, leading to delayed intervention and treatment. Additionally, seniors may be dealing with multiple chronic health conditions, which can complicate their recovery process and require specialized care.

Social isolation and loneliness are also prevalent among older adults, making it harder to find support systems and maintain motivation. Furthermore, the stigma surrounding substance abuse in seniors can hinder their willingness to seek help.

It is crucial for healthcare professionals, families, and society to be compassionate, knowledgeable, and understanding to provide the necessary support and guidance for seniors on their path to recovery.

Overlooked Demographic Group

Seniors, often overlooked in discussions about substance abuse, require a comprehensive guide to recovery that addresses their unique needs and challenges.

This overlooked demographic group faces a range of factors that contribute to substance abuse, including physical and mental health issues, social isolation, and the loss of loved ones.

Many seniors also struggle with the stigma associated with addiction, which can prevent them from seeking help or receiving the support they need.

It is important to recognize the specific vulnerabilities and barriers that seniors face to develop effective strategies for prevention and recovery.

A comprehensive guide that combines compassion, knowledge, and experience can provide essential information and resources tailored to seniors, helping them navigate the complexities of addiction and find the support they need to embark on a successful path to recovery.

Recovery Resources for Seniors

A comprehensive guide to recovery for seniors offers a wealth of resources and support tailored specifically to the unique needs and challenges faced by this often-overlooked demographic group.

Seniors struggling with substance abuse require specialized assistance that considers their age-related physical, cognitive, and emotional changes. Recovery resources for seniors encompass a range of options, including support groups, counseling services, and rehabilitation programs designed specifically for older adults.

These resources aim to provide a safe and understanding environment where seniors can explore the underlying causes of their addiction and develop coping strategies for maintaining sobriety. Additionally, recovery resources for seniors often include educational materials and workshops to increase awareness and understanding of addiction, as well as practical tools and tips for staying healthy and engaged in recovery.

Frequently Asked Questions

What Are Some Common Risk Factors for Substance Abuse Among Seniors?

Common risk factors for substance abuse among seniors include chronic pain, loneliness, loss of loved ones, retirement, and financial stress. These factors can contribute to increased vulnerability and the use of substances as a coping mechanism.

How Does Substance Abuse Impact the

Physical Health of Senior Citizens?

Substance abuse can have significant physical health impacts on senior citizens. It can lead to a range of issues such as organ damage, increased risk of falls and accidents, weakened immune system, and exacerbation of existing health conditions.

Are There Any Specific Warning Signs or Symptoms to Look Out for in Seniors Who May Be Struggling with Substance Abuse?

Warning signs and symptoms of substance abuse in seniors include changes in behavior, mood swings, unexplained injuries, or accidents, neglecting personal hygiene, withdrawal from social activities, and a decline in cognitive abilities. It is important to address these signs promptly and seek professional help.

What Are Some Effective Treatment Options for Seniors with Substance Abuse Issues?

Effective treatment options for seniors with substance abuse issues include individual and group therapy, medication-assisted treatment, and support groups. It is essential to tailor the treatment plan to the specific needs of the individual, considering their medical and mental health conditions.

How Can Family Members and Caregivers Support Seniors in Their Recovery Journey?

Family members and caregivers play a crucial role in supporting seniors in their recovery journey from substance abuse. By providing emotional support, encouraging healthy habits, and connecting them with appropriate resources, they can contribute to their loved one's successful rehabilitation.

Conclusion

In conclusion, addressing substance abuse among seniors is of utmost importance due to the unique challenges they face. By providing a comprehensive guide to recovery specifically tailored for seniors, this book aims to offer compassionate support and expert knowledge to help them overcome their addiction.

It is crucial to acknowledge the specific needs and experiences of senior citizens in order to effectively address substance abuse and promote a healthier and happier life for them.

CHAPTER 1: UNDERSTANDING SUBSTANCE ABUSE IN SENIORS

Substance abuse among seniors is a topic that demands our attention and understanding. As we embark on this journey of exploration, we will uncover the prevalence of substance abuse in the aging population, the risk factors that contribute to this alarming trend, and the common substances that are abused by seniors.

Additionally, we will explore the physical and mental health implications associated with substance abuse in older adults, as well as the impact of social isolation on their vulnerability to addiction.

By recognizing the signs of substance abuse in aging individuals, we can better equip ourselves to intervene and provide the necessary support. Join me as we unveil strategies for prevention and intervention in senior substance abuse, for the sake of their well-being and quality of life.

Key Takeaways
- Substance abuse among seniors is a significant issue that often goes unnoticed.
- Unique challenges faced by seniors, such as retirement, loss of loved ones, and declining physical

- Misuse of prescription medications is a growing problem among older adults.
- Loneliness and isolation play a significant role in driving seniors to turn to drugs or alcohol as a coping mechanism.

Prevalence of Substance Abuse in Seniors

As we explore the prevalence of substance abuse in seniors, it is crucial to approach this topic with empathy and understanding. Aging individuals may face unique challenges and vulnerabilities that contribute to their increased risk of addiction.

It is important to acknowledge that substance abuse among seniors is often hidden, making it even more critical to raise awareness and provide support.

Aging and Addiction Risks

Substance abuse among seniors is a significant concern that requires a compassionate and informed approach to understanding the prevalence of addiction risks in this population.

As individuals age, they often face numerous challenges that can increase their vulnerability to substance abuse. Retirement, loss of loved ones, and declining physical or mental health can lead to feelings of loneliness, depression, and anxiety, which may drive seniors to turn to drugs or alcohol as a coping mechanism.

Additionally, the misuse of prescription medications is a growing issue among older adults.

The prevalence of addiction risks in seniors is alarming, with studies showing that approximately 17% of adults aged 60 and older struggle with substance abuse.

It is crucial to address this issue with empathy, knowledge, and support, providing effective interventions and treatment options to ensure the well-being of our aging population.

Hidden Substance Abuse

Hidden within the senior population lies a concerning prevalence of substance abuse that demands our attention and compassionate understanding.

Contrary to widespread belief, substance abuse is not limited to the younger generations. In fact, the rate of substance abuse among seniors is on the rise, due to factors such as retirement, loss of loved ones, and chronic pain.

Many seniors turn to alcohol, prescription medications, or even illicit drugs to cope with these challenges. Unfortunately, this hidden epidemic often goes unnoticed, as symptoms of substance abuse in seniors can be mistaken for normal signs of aging.

It is crucial that we educate ourselves and the community about the signs and risks of substance abuse in seniors and offer support and resources to those in need.

Health Consequences and Risks

In the senior population, substance abuse poses significant health consequences and risks that require our attention and understanding. It is a commonly held misconception that substance abuse only affects younger individuals. However, as the population ages, the prevalence of substance abuse in seniors is increasing, and its impact on their health cannot be ignored.

Substance abuse can lead to a range of physical and mental health problems, including cardiovascular diseases, liver damage, cognitive impairment, and increased risk of falls and accidents. Additionally, substance abuse can worsen existing health conditions and interfere with the effectiveness of medications.

It is crucial for healthcare providers, caregivers, and society to recognize the unique challenges faced by seniors with substance abuse issues and provide them with the necessary support and resources for recovery.

Risk Factors for Substance Abuse in Aging Adults

As individuals age, there are several contributing factors that may increase their risk of developing substance abuse issues. These factors include social isolation, retirement, loss of loved ones, and chronic health conditions.

Additionally, aging adults may experience age-related vulnerabilities such as cognitive decline, loneliness, and a lack of purpose.

It is also important to consider the impact of chronic pain, as seniors may turn to substances as a way to cope with their physical discomfort.

Understanding these risk factors is crucial in developing effective prevention and intervention strategies to support aging adults in maintaining their health and well-being.

Contributing Factors to Senior Substance Abuse

The prevalence of substance abuse among aging adults can be attributed to a complex interplay of various risk factors, necessitating a thorough understanding of the contributing factors involved. When it comes to senior substance abuse, the following factors can contribute to the problem:

- **Physical health issues**: Chronic pain, disabilities, and other health conditions can lead seniors to rely on medications, some of which can be addictive.
- **Mental health conditions**: Depression, anxiety, and loneliness can drive seniors to seek solace in substances.
- **Retirement and loss**: The transition to retirement

and the loss of loved ones can lead to feelings of purposelessness and grief, increasing the risk of substance abuse.
- **Social isolation**: Limited social interactions and reduced support networks can contribute to substance abuse as seniors may turn to substances as a coping mechanism.
- **Lack of knowledge and awareness**: Many seniors may not be aware of the potential risks associated with substance abuse or the available resources for help.

Understanding these contributing factors is crucial in developing effective prevention and intervention strategies to support aging adults in overcoming substance abuse.

Age-Related Vulnerabilities

Understanding the unique vulnerabilities that aging adults face can shed light on the risk factors associated with substance abuse in this population.

As individuals age, they often experience significant life changes, such as retirement, loss of loved ones, and declining physical health. These changes can lead to feelings of isolation, depression, and anxiety, making seniors more susceptible to turning to substances as a coping mechanism.

Moreover, age-related physiological changes can alter the way medications and substances are processed by the body, increasing the risk of dependency and adverse reactions.

Additionally, older adults may face limited social support systems, financial hardships, and lack of access to appropriate healthcare, further exacerbating their vulnerability to substance abuse.

It is crucial for healthcare professionals, caregivers, and society as a whole to recognize and address these age-related vulnerabilities in order to effectively prevent and treat substance abuse in aging adults.

Impact of Chronic Pain

Chronic pain can significantly contribute to the risk of substance abuse in aging adults, necessitating a comprehensive understanding and compassionate approach to address this complex issue. Seniors experiencing chronic pain often find themselves in a vulnerable position, where they are desperate for relief and may turn to substances as a means of escape.

The impact of chronic pain on substance abuse in aging adults is multifaceted and requires careful consideration. Here are some key points to understand:

- Chronic pain can lead to increased reliance on pain medications, increasing the risk of substance abuse.
- Seniors with chronic pain may feel isolated and hopeless, seeking solace in substances to cope with their emotional distress.
- The use of substances to manage pain can create a vicious cycle, exacerbating both the physical and emotional aspects of chronic pain.
- Untreated chronic pain can negatively affect a senior's quality of life, leading to depression and anxiety, which can further contribute to substance abuse.
- A multidisciplinary approach that combines pain management strategies, psychological support, and social engagement is crucial in addressing chronic pain and reducing the risk of substance abuse in aging adults.

Common Substances Abused by Seniors

Substance abuse among seniors is a complex issue that requires our understanding and support.

It is important to acknowledge that alcohol misuse is a prevalent problem among aging adults, often leading to serious health complications.

Additionally, prescription medication misuse and illicit drug use are also common substances of abuse that require our attention and intervention.

Alcohol and Aging

As individuals age, the relationship between alcohol and its effects becomes increasingly complex, requiring a nuanced understanding of the challenges faced by seniors in relation to substance abuse. It is crucial to approach the topic of alcohol and aging with empathy and knowledge, supporting seniors in their journey towards healthier habits.

Here are some key points to consider:

- **Physiological changes**: Aging affects how the body processes alcohol, leading to increased sensitivity and slower metabolism.
- **Medication interactions**: Alcohol can interact negatively with various medications commonly prescribed to seniors, resulting in adverse effects.
- **Increased vulnerability**: Seniors may experience social isolation, grief, or chronic pain, which can contribute to alcohol misuse as a coping mechanism.
- **Health consequences**: Excessive alcohol consumption in older adults can lead to cognitive impairment, falls, liver damage, and an increased risk of developing chronic diseases.
- **Treatment options**: Tailored interventions, including counseling, support groups, and medication management, can help seniors address alcohol-related concerns and improve their overall well-being.

Prescription Medication Misuse

Misuse of prescription medications is a significant concern among seniors, necessitating a compassionate and informed approach to address the complex challenges faced by this vulnerable population.

As individuals age, they may find themselves managing multiple health conditions, leading to an increased reliance on prescription medications. While these medications are meant to improve the quality of life, they can also be misused, leading to adverse effects. Seniors may accidentally take the wrong dosage or mix medications that should not be combined.

Additionally, some may intentionally misuse prescription medications to alleviate pain or cope with emotional distress. It is crucial for healthcare professionals, caregivers, and family members to provide support and education to seniors regarding the proper use of their medications.

Illicit Drug Use

Illicit drug use among seniors is a concerning issue that requires a compassionate and informed approach to address the unique challenges faced by this vulnerable population. The use of illicit drugs by seniors can have severe consequences on their physical and mental health, as well as their overall quality of life. Understanding the reasons behind illicit drug use in seniors is crucial for developing effective prevention and treatment strategies.

Some common substances abused by seniors include:

- **Marijuana**: Seniors may turn to marijuana for pain relief or relaxation, not realizing the potential risks and interactions with other medications.
- **Cocaine**: Although less common among seniors, cocaine abuse can lead to serious heart problems and other health complications.
- **Heroin**: Seniors may misuse heroin due to feelings of loneliness or depression, unaware of the considerable risk of overdose and addiction.
- **Methamphetamine**: Older adults may use

methamphetamine for increased energy or weight loss, but this can lead to severe health issues and dependency.
- **Prescription opioids**: Some seniors turn to illegally obtained prescription opioids for pain management, which can result in addiction and overdose.

Compassionate support and education are essential to help seniors navigate these challenges and live healthier, more fulfilling lives.

Physical and Mental Health Implications of Substance Abuse in Seniors

Substance abuse in seniors can have significant physical and mental health implications. Engaging in substance abuse puts seniors at risk of various health complications and consequences, including organ damage, weakened immune system, and increased vulnerability to falls and accidents.

Moreover, substance abuse can lead to cognitive impairment, worsening memory and concentration, and can even develop into addiction, further exacerbating the negative impact on overall well-being.

Health Risks and Consequences

As individuals age, the misuse of certain substances can have detrimental effects on their physical and mental well-being. It is important to understand the health risks and consequences associated with substance abuse in seniors. Here are some key points to consider:

Physical Health Implications:
- Increased risk of falls and injuries
- Worsening of existing medical conditions
- Impaired immune system function
- Liver damage and kidney dysfunction
- Cardiovascular problems such as high blood pressure

and heart disease

Mental Health Implications:
- Increased risk of depression and anxiety
- Cognitive decline and memory problems
- Higher likelihood of developing dementia or Alzheimer's disease
- Social isolation and withdrawal from activities
- Impaired decision-making and judgment

Cognitive Impairment and Addiction

The misuse of certain substances in seniors can lead to cognitive impairment, exacerbating both the physical and mental health implications of substance abuse.

Cognitive impairment refers to a decline in mental processes such as memory, attention, and decision-making. Substance abuse can worsen cognitive impairment in seniors due to the toxic effects of drugs or alcohol on the brain.

Additionally, long-term substance abuse can cause structural and functional changes in the brain, further impairing cognitive function. This can result in difficulties with daily activities, increased risk of accidents, and decreased quality of life.

It is crucial to address both substance abuse and cognitive impairment in seniors to ensure comprehensive and effective treatment. By providing support, education, and appropriate interventions, we can help seniors regain control of their lives and improve their overall well-being.

Impact on Physical Well-Being

Seniors who engage in substance abuse may experience significant negative effects on their physical well-being, impacting both their physical and mental health. It is crucial to understand the potential consequences that substance abuse can have on the aging population.

Here are some ways in which substance abuse can affect seniors' physical well-being:

- Increased risk of falls and injuries due to impaired balance and coordination.
- Decline in overall physical health, leading to chronic conditions such as heart disease, liver damage, and respiratory problems.
- Weakened immune system, making seniors more susceptible to infections and illnesses.
- Nutritional deficiencies due to poor appetite or improper diet, leading to weight loss and malnutrition.
- Negative impact on medication effectiveness, potentially interfering with the treatment of other health conditions.

Social Isolation and Substance Abuse in Older Adults

Social isolation can have a profound impact on the mental well-being of older adults. It increases their vulnerability to substance abuse. The experience of loneliness and isolation can lead to a vicious cycle. Individuals may turn to drugs or alcohol as a means of coping with their feelings of loneliness.

It is crucial for healthcare professionals to recognize the link between social isolation and substance abuse in older adults. They should provide the necessary support and resources to address these issues effectively.

Loneliness and Addiction

Loneliness and addiction can have a profound impact on the well-being and quality of life of older adults. As we age, we may experience loss of loved ones, retire from work, or face health challenges, leading to feelings of isolation and loneliness. Unfortunately, some individuals turn to substances to cope with these emotions, which can further exacerbate the problem.

Here are some key points to understand about the relationship between loneliness and addiction in older adults:

- Loneliness can increase the risk of substance abuse in seniors.
- Substance abuse can intensify feelings of loneliness and isolation.
- Older adults may turn to alcohol or prescription medication to ease their loneliness.
- Loneliness and addiction can create a vicious cycle, making it harder to break free from substance abuse.
- Seeking support, building meaningful connections, and engaging in activities can help combat loneliness and reduce the risk of addiction.

Understanding the impact of loneliness and addiction is crucial to developing effective strategies to support older adults in maintaining their well-being and quality of life.

Impact of Isolation

Isolation can have a significant impact on the mental and emotional well-being of older adults, potentially leading to an increased risk of substance abuse.

As individuals age, they may face various challenges that contribute to feelings of isolation, such as the loss of a spouse or loved ones, retirement, or physical limitations. These factors can all contribute to a sense of loneliness and disconnection from others, which can be incredibly distressing.

The lack of social interaction and support can leave seniors vulnerable to turning to substances as a means of coping with their feelings of isolation.

It is important to recognize and address the impact of isolation on older adults, providing them with the necessary support, companionship, and resources to combat these feelings and reduce the risk of substance abuse.

Elderly Substance Abuse

As older adults face various challenges that contribute to a sense of disconnection and loneliness, it is crucial to understand the potential link between these feelings and an increased risk of substance abuse in this population. The combination of social isolation and substance abuse can have a devastating impact on the physical and mental well-being of older adults.

Here are some key points to consider:

- Social isolation can lead to feelings of depression and anxiety, which may drive older adults to turn to substances as a coping mechanism.
- Older adults who are socially isolated may have limited access to support systems, making it more difficult for them to seek help for substance abuse.
- Substance abuse can exacerbate existing health conditions in older adults, leading to a decline in overall health and functioning.
- The stigma surrounding substance abuse in older adults can prevent them from seeking treatment or disclosing their struggles to healthcare professionals.
- Healthcare providers and caregivers should be vigilant in recognizing the signs of substance abuse in older adults and providing appropriate support and intervention.

Understanding the unique challenges faced by older adults and addressing the social isolation that often accompanies aging can help prevent and address substance abuse in this vulnerable population.

Recognizing the Signs of Substance Abuse in Aging Individuals

Recognizing the signs of substance abuse in aging individuals is crucial for early intervention and support. Seniors may exhibit warning signs such as sudden mood swings, social withdrawal, or neglecting personal hygiene.

Behavioral changes, such as increased secrecy or changes in sleep patterns, can also indicate substance abuse. Additionally, physical symptoms like unexplained weight loss, frequent falls, or memory problems should not be overlooked.

Warning Signs in Seniors

Seniors who may be struggling with substance abuse often exhibit subtle behavioral changes and physical symptoms that require keen observation and understanding. It is important to recognize these warning signs in order to provide the necessary support and intervention.

Here are some key indicators to look out for:

- Increased secrecy or withdrawal from family and friends.
- Drastic changes in appetite, weight loss or gain.
- Neglecting personal hygiene and appearance.
- Memory problems and confusion.
- Unexplained injuries or accidents.

These signs may vary from person to person, and it is crucial to approach the situation with empathy and understanding.

Substance abuse in seniors is a complex issue that often goes unnoticed, but by being vigilant and recognizing these warning signs, we can help our aging loved ones access the care and support they need.

Behavioral Changes Indicating Abuse

When observing the subtle behavioral changes and physical symptoms in seniors struggling with substance abuse, it is crucial to pay attention to the key indicators that suggest a need for support and intervention. Substance abuse can manifest in various ways in aging individuals, often leading to significant changes in their behavior.

These changes can include sudden mood swings, increased irritability or agitation, withdrawal from social activities, neglecting personal hygiene, and a decline in overall physical health. Family members and caregivers should be vigilant in recognizing these signs and reaching out for help.

It is important to approach the situation with empathy and understanding, as substance abuse can often be a coping mechanism for underlying issues such as chronic pain, loneliness, or depression. By addressing these behavioral changes and providing the necessary support, we can help seniors regain control of their lives and improve their overall well-being.

Physical Symptoms to Watch for

As individuals age, it becomes increasingly important to be aware of the physical symptoms that may indicate substance abuse in older adults. Recognizing these signs is crucial to provide the necessary support and intervention for those who may be struggling with substance abuse.

Here are some physical symptoms to watch for:

- Sudden weight loss or gain
- Noticeable changes in appearance or personal hygiene
- Frequent accidents or injuries
- Chronic pain or unexplained physical ailments
- Slurred speech or impaired coordination

These physical symptoms can be indicators of underlying substance abuse issues in seniors. It is important to approach the topic with empathy and understanding, as substance abuse can be a complex issue influenced by a range of factors.

Strategies for Prevention and Intervention in Senior Substance Abuse

Preventing and intervening in senior substance abuse requires a comprehensive approach that addresses the unique risk factors faced by older adults.

Early detection and screening are crucial in identifying potential substance abuse problems and initiating timely interventions.

Providing support and treatment options tailored to the needs of seniors can promote recovery and improve their overall well-being.

Risk Factors for Seniors

One key aspect in addressing senior substance abuse is understanding the various risk factors that contribute to this issue. Substance abuse among seniors can stem from a variety of factors, including:

- **Chronic pain**: Seniors who experience chronic pain may turn to substances to cope with their discomfort.
- **Loneliness and isolation**: Feelings of loneliness and isolation can lead seniors to seek solace in drugs or alcohol.
- **Mental health conditions**: Depression, anxiety, and other mental health conditions can increase vulnerability to substance abuse.
- **Loss and grief**: The loss of a spouse, friends, or independence can trigger substance abuse as a means of escape or self-medication.
- **Prescription medications**: Seniors may unintentionally become dependent on prescription medications due to prolonged use or improper dosage.

Recognizing these risk factors is crucial in developing effective prevention and intervention strategies for senior substance abuse. By addressing these underlying issues, we can help seniors lead healthier, happier lives.

Early Detection and Screening

Early detection and screening play a crucial role in preventing and intervening in senior substance abuse. It is important to recognize the signs and symptoms of substance abuse in seniors to ensure timely intervention and support.

Detecting substance abuse in seniors can be challenging as it may be mistaken for normal signs of aging or medical conditions. However, by implementing comprehensive screening measures, healthcare professionals can identify potential substance abuse problems early on.

Screening tools such as questionnaires and interviews can be used to assess substance use patterns, identify risk factors, and evaluate the need for further assessment or treatment. Additionally, regular screenings can help in monitoring treatment progress and identifying any relapse.

Early detection and screening are essential steps towards addressing substance abuse in seniors and promoting their overall well-being.

Support and Treatment Options

Support and treatment options are essential for addressing substance abuse in seniors and promoting their overall well-being. When it comes to helping seniors struggling with substance abuse, there are several options available. Here are some strategies that can be effective in supporting and treating seniors with substance abuse issues:

- **Support groups**: Encouraging seniors to join support groups can provide them with a safe and understanding space to share their experiences, learn from others, and receive emotional support.
- **Counseling**: Individual or group counseling sessions can help seniors explore the underlying causes of their substance abuse and develop strategies for coping with cravings and triggers.

- **Medication management**: For seniors who require medication for their substance abuse treatment, ensuring proper medication management and monitoring is crucial.
- **Inpatient or outpatient treatment programs**: These programs offer a structured environment with professional support, helping seniors detoxify and develop healthier habits.
- **Collaborative care**: Coordinating care between healthcare providers, family members, and other support systems can enhance the effectiveness of treatment and provide comprehensive support for seniors.

Frequently Asked Questions

What Are the Long-Term Effects of Substance Abuse on the Physical and Mental Health of Seniors?

Substance abuse in seniors can have significant long-term effects on both their physical and mental health. It can lead to chronic health conditions, cognitive decline, increased risk of falls and accidents, and worsen existing mental health issues.

What Are Some Common Misconceptions or Stereotypes About Substance Abuse in Older Adults?

Common misconceptions and stereotypes about substance abuse in older adults include if they do not engage in such behavior, dismissing their substance abuse as a result of aging, and underestimating the impact it can have on their physical and mental health.

How Does Social Isolation Contribute to Substance Abuse in Seniors?

Social isolation can contribute to substance abuse in seniors by creating feelings of loneliness, boredom, and depression. Without social connections and support, older adults may turn to drugs or alcohol as a coping mechanism, leading to increased risk of addiction and other health problems.

What Are Some Strategies for Effectively Communicating with and Supporting Seniors Who May Be Struggling with Substance Abuse?

Some strategies for effectively communicating with and supporting seniors who may be struggling with substance abuse include active listening, empathy, non-judgmental attitude, providing resources, and involving their support network in the recovery process.

Are There Any Specific Cultural or Socioeconomic Factors That Contribute to Substance Abuse in Older Adults?

Cultural and socioeconomic factors can contribute to substance abuse in older adults. These factors may include societal norms, access to healthcare, poverty, stress, and isolation. Understanding these factors is crucial in providing effective support and intervention.

Conclusion

In conclusion, substance abuse among seniors is a prevalent issue that can have significant physical and mental health implications.

Recognizing the signs of substance abuse in aging individuals is crucial for early intervention and prevention.

It is important to address the risk factors and provide support to prevent social isolation, which can contribute to substance abuse in older adults.

By implementing effective strategies for prevention and intervention, we can help seniors maintain their well-being and lead healthier lives.

CHAPTER 2: RECOGNIZING THE SIGNS OF SUBSTANCE ABUSE AND SEEKING HELP

As the population ages, it is essential to address the often-overlooked issue of substance abuse in seniors. Chapter 2 investigates the critical topic of recognizing the signs of substance abuse in older adults and the importance of seeking help.

By understanding the common indicators, both physical and behavioral, we can better identify those struggling with substance abuse. Furthermore, exploring the emotional and psychological symptoms associated with substance abuse in seniors will shed light on the complexities of this issue.

This chapter provides guidance on the necessary steps to take to support and help seniors who are battling substance abuse.

Key Takeaways

- Unexplained weight loss or gain, changes in sleep patterns, poor hygiene, increased secrecy, sudden mood swings, changes in appetite, unexplained bruises, or injuries, and decline in personal grooming and hygiene are signs and symptoms of substance

abuse in seniors.
- Substance abuse in seniors can lead to strained relationships with family, friends, and caregivers, withdrawal from social activities, feelings of loneliness and depression, exacerbation of existing mental health conditions, and development of anxiety, depression, and cognitive impairment.
- Physical indicators of substance abuse in older adults include changes in appetite, unexplained bruises or injuries, poor hygiene habits, cluttered and dirty living space, and strong body odor and oral health issues.
- Seeking help for substance abuse in seniors involves recognizing warning signs, consulting healthcare professionals for guidance and support, exploring treatment options tailored to the unique needs of older individuals, considering any co-existing medical conditions or medications, and seeking professional help to determine the underlying cause and provide appropriate treatment and support.

Common Signs of Substance Abuse in Seniors

Substance abuse can have distinct physical manifestations in seniors, such as unexplained weight loss or gain, changes in sleep patterns, and poor hygiene.

Additionally, behavioral changes like increased secrecy, sudden mood swings, and neglecting responsibilities may indicate substance abuse.

Moreover, seniors struggling with substance abuse often experience social and emotional consequences, including isolation, strained relationships, and a decline in overall well-being.

Recognizing these common signs is crucial in identifying and addressing substance abuse in seniors.

Physical Changes and Symptoms

As seniors age, they may experience physical changes and symptoms that can indicate substance abuse. It is important to be aware of these signs to identify and address the issue promptly.

Some physical changes that may be observed include changes in appetite, weight loss or gain, and unexplained bruises or injuries. Seniors may also exhibit changes in sleep patterns, such as insomnia or excessive drowsiness. Additionally, substance abuse can lead to changes in coordination and balance, resulting in falls or accidents.

Other symptoms that may be present include bloodshot eyes, dilated or constricted pupils, and a decline in personal grooming and hygiene. It is crucial to approach these physical changes and symptoms with empathy and seek professional help to address any underlying substance abuse issues.

Behavioral Changes and Patterns

Recognizing behavioral changes and patterns can provide valuable insights into potential substance abuse among seniors. It is essential to pay attention to any noticeable shifts in their usual behaviors and routines.

Seniors struggling with substance abuse may exhibit mood swings, irritability, or sudden changes in their social activities. They may become more isolated, withdrawing from family and friends. Additionally, their personal hygiene and appearance may deteriorate, and they may display forgetfulness or confusion. Financial difficulties, such as unexplained expenses or unpaid bills, can also be indicative of substance abuse.

It is important to approach these changes with empathy and understanding, as substance abuse in seniors is often driven by underlying issues such as chronic pain, loneliness, or depression. By recognizing these behavioral changes and patterns, we can help seniors seek the appropriate support and treatment they need.

Social and Emotional Impact

When observing the behavioral changes and patterns among seniors, it becomes evident that substance abuse can have a significant social and emotional impact on their lives.

The social and emotional consequences of substance abuse in seniors can be devastating, affecting their relationships, mental health, and overall well-being.

Seniors who struggle with substance abuse often experience strained relationships with family, friends, and caregivers. They may withdraw from social activities and isolate themselves, leading to feelings of loneliness and depression.

Substance abuse can also exacerbate existing mental health conditions or contribute to the development of new ones. Anxiety, depression, and cognitive impairment are common emotional consequences that seniors may experience.

Understanding the social and emotional impact of substance abuse in seniors is crucial to provide appropriate support and intervention.

Physical Indicators of Substance Abuse in Older Adults

When it comes to recognizing substance abuse in older adults, there are several physical indicators that may suggest a problem. Changes in appetite, such as sudden weight loss or gain, can be a sign of substance abuse.

Unexplained bruises or injuries may also be a red flag, as they could indicate falls or accidents related to impaired judgment or coordination.

Additionally, poor hygiene habits, such as neglecting personal grooming or wearing dirty clothes, may suggest a decline in self-care due to substance abuse.

It is important to be aware of these physical indicators and seek help if you suspect a loved one may be struggling with substance abuse.

Changes in Appetite

Changes in appetite can be a significant physical indicator of substance abuse in older adults. It is important to understand that substance abuse can affect a person's appetite in many ways.

Some individuals may experience a loss of appetite, resulting in significant weight loss and malnourishment. On the other hand, others may have an increased appetite and show signs of overeating or binge eating.

These changes in appetite can be attributed to the effects of substances on the brain and body. For example, certain drugs can suppress the appetite, while others may increase cravings for food.

It is crucial to recognize these changes and seek help for older adults who may be struggling with substance abuse. By addressing the underlying issue, healthcare professionals can provide appropriate treatment and support to improve their overall well-being.

Unexplained Bruises or Injuries

Substance abuse in older adults can manifest in various physical indicators. One significant clue to look out for is the presence of unexplained bruises or injuries. While occasional accidents and falls are common in older adults, frequent unexplained bruises or injuries may indicate substance abuse. These bruises may appear on various parts of the body and can range in severity from minor marks to more significant injuries.

It is important to approach this issue with empathy and understanding, as substance abuse in older adults is often overlooked or misinterpreted as a natural consequence of aging. If you notice unexplained bruises or injuries in an older adult, it is essential to address the situation with compassion and encourage them to seek medical attention and support to determine the underlying cause and provide appropriate interventions.

Poor Hygiene Habits

One physical indicator of substance abuse in older adults is poor hygiene habits, which can serve as a telltale sign of underlying substance misuse. When seniors struggle with substance abuse, their personal care and hygiene often take a backseat. Neglected grooming, lack of regular bathing, unkempt appearance, and disheveled hair are common signs of poor hygiene habits in seniors struggling with substance abuse.

Another indicator is strong body odor. Frequent substance use can lead to neglecting personal hygiene, resulting in a strong and persistent smell. Additionally, substance abuse can negatively impact oral health, causing issues like tooth decay, gum disease, and bad breath.

Furthermore, the living space of an older adult battling substance abuse may be cluttered, dirty, and filled with empty bottles or drug paraphernalia. This dirty and neglected living environment can further indicate poor hygiene habits.

It is important to approach this topic with empathy and understanding, as poor hygiene habits can indicate deeper issues that require professional help and support.

Behavioral Changes Associated with Substance Abuse in Seniors

When it comes to substance abuse in seniors, there are several behavioral changes to be aware of.

One common indicator is mood swings, where individuals may experience extreme highs and lows.

Social withdrawal is another behavioral change, as seniors may isolate themselves from friends and family.

Increased secrecy is also a red flag, as seniors may become more guarded about their activities and whereabouts.

Recognizing these behavioral changes is crucial in identifying substance abuse in seniors and seeking the appropriate help and support they need.

Mood Swings

Seniors experiencing substance abuse may exhibit noticeable mood swings that can impact their overall well-being and quality of life. Recognizing these mood swings is crucial in identifying potential substance abuse issues and seeking appropriate help and support.

Here are some common signs of mood swings in seniors struggling with substance abuse:

- Extreme irritability or anger outbursts, even in situations that typically would not warrant such reactions.
- Unexplained and sudden bouts of sadness or depression, often lasting for extended periods.
- Rapid shifts in mood, going from euphoria to extreme agitation or sadness within a short span of time.
- Increased isolation and withdrawal from social activities and relationships, preferring to be alone rather than engaging with others.

It is important to approach seniors experiencing mood swings with empathy and understanding, encouraging them to seek professional help and support to address their substance abuse issues effectively.

Social Withdrawal

Social withdrawal is a common behavioral change observed in seniors struggling with substance abuse. When seniors begin to withdraw socially, they may start avoiding social gatherings, isolating themselves from friends and family, and losing interest in activities they once enjoyed. This withdrawal can be a result of the shame or guilt associated with their substance abuse, or it may be a consequence of the physical and mental effects of the substances themselves.

Seniors may feel embarrassed, or fear being judged by others, leading them to retreat from social interactions. It is essential to approach seniors with empathy and understanding, as social withdrawal can further exacerbate their substance abuse issues. Encouraging open communication and providing support can help seniors regain their sense of connection and reduce the risk of further isolation.

Increased Secrecy

Amidst the challenges faced by seniors struggling with substance abuse, another notable behavioral change often observed is an increased level of secrecy. This secrecy can manifest in numerous ways and is often a result of the shame, guilt, or fear associated with their substance abuse.

Seniors may go to great lengths to hide their addiction from loved ones and healthcare professionals, which can make it even more difficult to recognize and address the problem. Some common signs of increased secrecy in seniors with substance abuse issues include:

- Frequently locking doors and windows
- Refusing visitors or social engagements
- Being overly protective of personal belongings
- Exhibiting secretive or suspicious behavior

It is important for family members, friends, and healthcare professionals to be vigilant and compassionate when dealing with seniors who exhibit these signs. Creating a safe and supportive environment can encourage them to open and seek the help they need to overcome their substance abuse.

Emotional and Psychological Symptoms of Substance Abuse in Older Individuals

Substance abuse in older individuals can lead to a range of emotional and psychological symptoms.

One common symptom is mood swings and irritability, where the individual may experience sudden changes in their emotional state and become easily agitated.

Increased anxiety and depression are also prevalent, as substance abuse can exacerbate existing mental health conditions or trigger new ones.

Additionally, cognitive impairment and confusion may occur, affecting memory, attention, and decision-making abilities.

It is crucial to recognize these symptoms and seek help to address the underlying substance abuse issue and improve the individual's overall well-being.

Mood Swings and Irritability

As individuals age, they may experience an increased vulnerability to mood swings and irritability, which can be indicators of emotional and psychological symptoms associated with substance abuse. It is important for caregivers, family members, and healthcare professionals to recognize these signs and take appropriate action.

Here are some key points to understand about mood swings and irritability in seniors:

- Mood swings and irritability can be caused by various factors, including the use of substances such as alcohol, prescription drugs, or illicit drugs.
- Substance abuse can disrupt the brain's natural balance of chemicals, leading to changes in mood and behavior.
- Seniors may be more prone to mood swings and irritability due to underlying health conditions, medication interactions, or social isolation.
- It is crucial to approach seniors with empathy

and understanding, as they may be facing unique challenges related to aging and substance abuse.

Increased Anxiety and Depression

Older individuals who are experiencing increased anxiety and depression may be exhibiting emotional and psychological symptoms associated with substance abuse. It is important to recognize that anxiety and depression can be common in older adults due to numerous factors such as health issues, loss of loved ones, or social isolation.

However, when these symptoms become more pronounced and persistent, it could be an indication of substance abuse. Substance abuse can worsen anxiety and depression symptoms, leading to a vicious cycle of self-medication.

It is crucial to approach this issue with empathy and understanding. Encouraging open communication and providing support can help older individuals feel comfortable in seeking help. Professional assistance from healthcare providers or addiction specialists should be sought to address the underlying causes of anxiety and depression and provide appropriate treatment and support.

Cognitive Impairment and Confusion

Recognizing the potential signs of substance abuse in seniors requires an understanding of the emotional and psychological symptoms that may manifest, such as cognitive impairment and confusion. These symptoms can often be mistaken for normal aging or other medical conditions. It is crucial to be aware of the following indicators:

- **Memory problems**: Seniors experiencing substance abuse may struggle with memory loss or have difficulty recalling recent events or conversations.
- **Confusion and disorientation**: They may appear mentally foggy or have trouble concentrating and making decisions.

- **Slowed thinking and reaction time**: Substance abuse can impact cognitive functions, leading to slowed thinking and delayed responses.
- **Poor judgment and decision-making**: Seniors may make impulsive and risky choices due to impaired judgment.

If you notice any of these signs in yourself or a loved one, it is essential to seek professional help to determine the underlying cause and provide appropriate treatment and support.

Steps to Take in Seeking Help for Seniors Struggling with Substance Abuse

When it comes to seeking help for seniors struggling with substance abuse, there are several important steps to take.

The first step is to recognize the warning signs, such as changes in behavior, physical health issues, and social withdrawal.

Once these signs are identified, it is crucial to consult healthcare professionals who can provide guidance and support.

Finally, it is essential to explore treatment options that are specifically tailored to the unique needs of older individuals, taking into account any co-existing medical conditions or medications.

Recognizing Warning Signs

Are you concerned about the well-being of a senior in your life and suspect they may be struggling with substance abuse? Recognizing the warning signs is crucial in helping them seek the necessary support.

Here are some signs to look out for:

- **Physical changes**: Unexplained weight loss, frequent bruises, bloodshot eyes, and poor hygiene.
- **Behavioral changes**: Increased secrecy, withdrawal from social activities, sudden mood swings, and unexplained financial problems.

- **Neglecting responsibilities**: Missing appointments, neglecting personal and household responsibilities, and a decline in performance at work or school.
- **Health issues**: Chronic pain, memory problems, and increased susceptibility to illnesses.

It is important to approach the situation with empathy and understanding. Remember, substance abuse is a complex issue, and the senior may need professional help to overcome it. Encourage open dialogue and offer support in seeking appropriate treatment options.

Consulting Healthcare Professionals

One crucial step in seeking help for seniors struggling with substance abuse is consulting healthcare professionals who specialize in addiction and geriatric care. These professionals have the expertise and experience to accurately assess the situation and provide appropriate guidance and treatment options.

When consulting healthcare professionals, it is important to be open and honest about the senior's substance abuse history, symptoms, and any other relevant information. The healthcare professional will conduct a thorough evaluation, which may include physical exams, laboratory tests, and psychological assessments. They will also consider the senior's overall health and any other medical conditions they may have.

Based on this evaluation, the healthcare professional will develop a personalized treatment plan that may include medication, therapy, support groups, or a combination of these. It is essential to involve healthcare professionals to ensure the best possible care and support for seniors struggling with substance abuse.

Exploring Treatment Options

Exploring treatment options is a crucial step in seeking help for seniors struggling with substance abuse. It allows for personalized care and support tailored to their specific needs. When considering treatment options, it is important to remember that everyone's journey towards recovery is unique.

Here are some options to consider:

- **Inpatient Rehabilitation**: This involves staying at a facility where seniors receive around-the-clock care and support. It provides a structured environment to focus on recovery.
- **Outpatient Programs**: These programs allow seniors to receive treatment while living at home. They offer flexibility and allow individuals to continue with their daily activities.
- **Support Groups**: Joining support groups, such as Alcoholics Anonymous or Narcotics Anonymous, can provide seniors with a sense of community and understanding from others who have faced similar challenges.
- **Counseling or Therapy**: Individual or group therapy sessions can help seniors address underlying issues contributing to their substance abuse and develop healthier coping mechanisms.

Frequently Asked Questions

What Are Some Common Misconceptions About Substance Abuse in Seniors?

Common misconceptions about substance abuse in seniors include the belief that older adults are not at risk or that their symptoms are a normal part of aging. It is crucial to recognize the signs and seek help to ensure their well-being.

How Does Substance Abuse in Seniors Differ from Substance Abuse in Younger Individuals?

Substance abuse in seniors differs from that in younger individuals due to unique factors such as physical health conditions, medication interactions, and social isolation.

Understanding these differences is crucial in providing effective support and treatment for this vulnerable population.

What Are Some Potential Underlying Causes or Risk Factors for Substance Abuse in Seniors?

Substance abuse in seniors can be influenced by various underlying causes and risk factors. These include chronic pain, loneliness, grief, loss, retirement, and the presence of co-occurring mental health disorders. Identifying these factors is crucial for effective intervention and support.

Are There Any Specific Challenges or Barriers That Seniors Face When Seeking Help for Substance Abuse?

Seniors face unique challenges and barriers when seeking help for substance abuse. These may include stigma, lack of awareness or knowledge about available resources, fear of judgment or loss of independence, and physical or cognitive limitations that affect their ability to access treatment.

What Are Some Resources or Support Systems Available Specifically for Seniors Struggling with Substance Abuse?

There are various resources and support systems available specifically for seniors struggling with substance abuse, including specialized treatment programs, counseling services, support groups, and helplines. These resources aim to provide guidance, assistance, and understanding for seniors in need.

Conclusion

In conclusion, it is crucial to recognize the signs of substance abuse in seniors and take the necessary steps to seek help for them.

By identifying physical indicators, behavioral changes, and emotional symptoms, we can better understand the challenges faced by older individuals struggling with substance abuse.

It is important to approach this issue with empathy and provide support through professional interventions.

With proper treatment and support, seniors can regain their health and well-being, leading to a better quality of life.

CHAPTER 3: CREATING A SUPPORTIVE ENVIRONMENT

As society continues to grapple with the multifaceted issue of substance abuse, it is crucial that we do not overlook the specific challenges faced by seniors in this regard.

Chapter 3 examines the importance of creating a supportive environment for seniors struggling with substance abuse, recognizing their unique needs, and providing them with the necessary tools for recovery.

By understanding the physical and emotional aspects that come into play, as well as the importance of accessible and age-appropriate treatment options, we can begin to address this issue in a holistic and compassionate manner.

Join us as we explore the ways in which we can foster a safe and supportive space for seniors on their journey to wellness.

Key Takeaways
- Aging increases the risk of addiction in seniors due to factors like loneliness and loss of social connections.
- Seniors often face mental health challenges like depression and anxiety, which contribute to substance abuse.
- Physical health considerations, such as chronic pain and medical conditions, must be considered when providing care for seniors with substance abuse.

- Creating a safe and supportive physical environment, fostering emotional support and connection, and involving family members in the recovery process are crucial for creating a supportive environment for seniors with substance abuse.

Understanding the Unique Needs of Seniors

As we strive to create a supportive environment for seniors with substance abuse, it is crucial that we understand their unique needs. Aging brings about a range of factors that increase the risk of addiction, such as loneliness and loss of social connections.

Additionally, seniors often face mental health challenges like depression and anxiety, which can contribute to substance abuse. Furthermore, physical health considerations must be considered, as seniors may have chronic pain or medical conditions that require specialized care.

Aging and Addiction Risks

Seniors face unique challenges when it comes to addiction risks, highlighting the importance of understanding their distinct needs to create a supportive environment. As we age, our bodies and minds undergo significant changes, making seniors more vulnerable to substance abuse.

Here are three key factors that contribute to the increased addiction risks among seniors:

1. **Physical and mental health decline**: As we age, our physical health declines, and chronic pain becomes more prevalent. Seniors may turn to substances to alleviate pain or cope with the emotional toll of their declining health.
2. **Loneliness and isolation**: Many seniors experience feelings of loneliness and isolation, especially if they have lost loved ones or are living alone. Substance abuse can provide temporary relief from these

feelings, leading to a dangerous cycle of dependency.
3. **Medication misuse**: Seniors often take multiple medications to manage various health conditions. Unfortunately, this can increase the risk of medication misuse or mixing drugs with substances, resulting in harmful interactions and addiction.

Mental Health Challenges

With an understanding of the unique challenges that seniors face in relation to addiction risks, it is crucial to delve into the mental health challenges they encounter, as this plays a significant role in creating a supportive environment for them.

As seniors age, they often experience various mental health issues such as depression, anxiety, and cognitive decline. These challenges can contribute to substance abuse problems or worsen existing ones.

Depression, for example, can lead to self-medication with drugs or alcohol as a means of coping with feelings of sadness and hopelessness. Additionally, anxiety can make seniors more susceptible to developing substance abuse issues as they seek relief from their worries and fears.

Cognitive decline, on the other hand, can impair judgment and decision-making abilities, making it harder for seniors to recognize and address their substance abuse problems.

Understanding and addressing these mental health challenges is crucial in creating a supportive environment that promotes recovery and overall well-being for seniors struggling with substance abuse.

Physical Health Considerations

Understanding the unique physical health needs of older adults is essential when creating a supportive environment for seniors struggling with substance abuse. Older adults often face a range of physical health challenges, which can be exacerbated by substance abuse. It is crucial to address these considerations to ensure comprehensive care and support for this vulnerable population.

To evoke an emotional response in the audience, here are three key physical health considerations to keep in mind:

1. **Increased vulnerability**: Aging brings a natural decline in physical resilience, making older adults more susceptible to the harmful effects of substance abuse. Their bodies may struggle to metabolize drugs or alcohol, resulting in prolonged intoxication and increased health risks.
2. **Chronic conditions**: Older adults are more likely to have pre-existing medical conditions such as cardiovascular disease, diabetes, or arthritis. Substance abuse can worsen these conditions, leading to further complications and decreased quality of life.
3. **Medication interactions**: Many seniors take multiple medications to manage their health conditions. Substance abuse can interfere with these medications, leading to adverse reactions or reduced effectiveness in treating their medical conditions.

Creating a Safe and Secure Physical Environment

Creating a safe and secure physical environment is crucial for seniors with substance abuse.

Implementing safety measures such as installing handrails and grab bars can help prevent accidents and injuries.

Additionally, designing accessible spaces that are free of obstacles and hazards can ensure a supportive environment for seniors on their path to recovery.

Safety Measures for Seniors

Ensuring the safety and security of seniors in their physical environment is of utmost importance for maintaining their well-being and minimizing potential risks. Here are three crucial safety measures that can help create a safe and secure environment for seniors:

1. **Fall prevention**: Falls are a common cause of injuries among seniors. Implementing measures such as removing tripping hazards, installing grab bars in bathrooms, and improving lighting can significantly reduce the risk of falls.
2. **Medication management**: Seniors often take multiple medications, which can increase the risk of medication errors. Proper medication management includes organizing medications, using pill organizers, and involving healthcare professionals to ensure correct dosages and avoid potential interactions.
3. **Home security**: Seniors may be vulnerable to thefts or scams. Installing security systems, using door and window locks, and educating seniors about common scams can help protect them from potential harm.

Designing Accessible Spaces

Designing accessible spaces is essential for promoting the safety and security of seniors in their physical environment. As individuals age, their mobility and sensory abilities may decline, making it crucial to create spaces that accommodate their needs.

When designing accessible spaces for seniors with substance abuse, it is important to consider factors such as lighting, clear signage, and reduced clutter to minimize hazards and promote independence. Installing grab bars in bathrooms and stairways can provide much-needed support, while ramps and elevators can ensure easy access to different areas of the facility.

Additionally, incorporating non-slip flooring and wide doorways can prevent falls and accommodate mobility aids such as wheelchairs and walkers. By creating accessible spaces, we can help seniors with substance abuse feel safe, secure, and empowered in their environment.

Preventing Accidents and Injuries

To ensure the safety and well-being of seniors with substance abuse, it is crucial to establish a physical environment that minimizes the risk of accidents and injuries. Creating a safe and secure space not only provides a sense of comfort but also promotes a sense of trust and support.

Here are three essential measures to prevent accidents and injuries in the environment:

1. **Remove hazards**: Conduct a thorough assessment of the living area and remove any potential hazards such as loose rugs, cluttered walkways, and unstable furniture. This will reduce the risk of falls and other accidents.
2. **Adequate lighting**: Ensure that all areas are well-lit, especially hallways, staircases, and bathrooms. Adequate lighting enhances visibility and reduces the chances of tripping or falling.
3. **Assistive devices**: Install necessary assistive devices like handrails, grab bars, and non-slip mats in bathrooms and showers. This aid provides stability and support for seniors, reducing the risk of accidents.

Fostering Emotional Support and Connection

Fostering emotional support and connection is crucial in helping seniors with substance abuse issues.

Social engagement activities provide opportunities for seniors to interact with others and develop meaningful connections, reducing feelings of isolation and loneliness.

Peer support groups offer a safe space for seniors to share their experiences, gain support from others facing similar challenges, and learn coping strategies.

Additionally, involving family members in the recovery process can strengthen relationships, provide emotional support, and increase accountability.

Social Engagement Activities

Creating a supportive and engaging environment for seniors with substance abuse involves implementing social engagement activities that foster emotional support and connection. These activities not only provide a sense of belonging and purpose but also help individuals in their recovery journey.

Here are three social engagement activities that can evoke an emotional response in seniors with substance abuse:

1. **Support groups**: Participating in support groups allows seniors to connect with others who are facing similar challenges. This sense of camaraderie and shared experiences can provide comfort, encouragement, and a safe space for discussing their struggles and triumphs.
2. **Art therapy**: Engaging in creative activities such as painting, drawing, or sculpting can help seniors express their emotions and thoughts in a non-verbal way. Art therapy promotes self-discovery, emotional healing, and personal growth.
3. **Volunteer work**: Encouraging seniors to give back to their community through volunteer work can boost their self-esteem and sense of purpose. It also provides an opportunity to connect with others, develop new skills, and make a positive impact on society.

Peer Support Groups

One effective approach to fostering emotional support and connection among seniors with substance abuse is through the establishment of peer support groups. These groups provide a safe and understanding environment where seniors can connect with others who share similar experiences and challenges.

Peer support groups offer a sense of belonging and empathy, allowing individuals to feel heard and understood without judgment. Through regular meetings, participants can share their stories, exchange coping strategies, and provide emotional support to one another. This sense of community can be a powerful motivator for seniors in their journey towards recovery.

It is important to ensure that these support groups are facilitated by trained professionals who can guide discussions and provide resources, making sure that all participants feel supported and encouraged. Peer support groups can play a crucial role in fostering emotional well-being and resilience among seniors with substance abuse issues.

Family Involvement

Family involvement plays a crucial role in fostering emotional support and connection for seniors with substance abuse. When families are actively involved in the recovery process, it helps seniors feel loved, supported, and understood. Here are three ways in which family involvement can make a positive impact:

1. **Emotional support**: Seniors with substance abuse often struggle with feelings of guilt, shame, and isolation. Family members can provide a safe space for them to express their emotions without judgment. This emotional support can help seniors build resilience and cope with the challenges of recovery.
2. **Enhanced motivation**: Family involvement can serve as a powerful motivator for seniors to stay committed to their recovery journey. Knowing that their loved ones are invested in their well-being can provide seniors with the encouragement they need to overcome obstacles and maintain sobriety.
3. **Rebuilding relationships**: Substance abuse can

strain family relationships, leading to broken trust and communication breakdowns. Family involvement in the recovery process can help rebuild these relationships by fostering open and honest communication, rebuilding trust, and creating a supportive and loving environment.

Providing Accessible and Age-Appropriate Treatment Options

As we seek to support seniors with substance abuse issues, it is crucial to provide them with accessible and age-appropriate treatment options.

Tailored treatment programs can address their specific needs and challenges, considering factors such as their age, physical health, and cognitive abilities.

Specialized care facilities that cater to the unique needs of older adults can also play a significant role in ensuring their wellbeing.

Additionally, incorporating holistic therapeutic approaches that encompass physical, mental, and emotional aspects can contribute to their overall recovery and long-term success.

Tailored Treatment Programs

Tailored treatment programs address the unique needs of seniors with substance abuse by providing accessible and age-appropriate treatment options. These programs recognize that older adults may require specialized care due to their distinct physical, mental, and social circumstances.

Here are three essential elements of tailored treatment programs:

1. **Comprehensive assessment**: A thorough evaluation helps identify co-existing medical conditions, cognitive impairments, and social support systems. This information guides the development of

individualized treatment plans that consider the specific challenges faced by seniors.
2. **Integrated care**: By combining medical, psychiatric, and addiction treatment services, tailored programs ensure holistic care for seniors. This approach addresses not only substance abuse but also any underlying physical or mental health issues.
3. **Age-appropriate interventions**: Treatment programs for seniors incorporate age-specific approaches, such as cognitive-behavioral therapy adapted for older adults, support groups, and medication management. These strategies foster engagement, promote positive outcomes, and enhance the overall well-being of seniors.

Tailored treatment programs for seniors with substance abuse play a crucial role in providing the support and care necessary for their unique circumstances.

Specialized Care Facilities

Specialized care facilities provide accessible and age-appropriate treatment options for seniors struggling with substance abuse. These facilities are specifically designed to meet the unique needs of older adults, offering a supportive and understanding environment. Seniors may face different challenges when it comes to substance abuse, such as co-existing medical conditions or cognitive impairments. Specialized care facilities are equipped to manage these complexities, ensuring that seniors receive the care they need.

These facilities offer a range of treatment options, including detoxification, counseling, medication management, and holistic therapies. They also provide a sense of community, allowing seniors to connect with others who are going through similar experiences. Moreover, staff members in specialized care facilities are well-trained in geriatric care and substance abuse treatment, ensuring that seniors receive appropriate care and support.

Holistic Therapeutic Approaches

Holistic therapeutic approaches offer accessible and age-appropriate treatment options for seniors struggling with substance abuse. These approaches recognize that seniors have unique needs and require specialized care to address their physical, psychological, and emotional well-being. By taking a holistic approach, treatment providers can ensure that seniors receive comprehensive care that focuses on their individual needs and promotes overall wellness.

Here are three key benefits of holistic therapeutic approaches for seniors with substance abuse:

1. **Personalized treatment plans**: Holistic therapies take into account the specific needs and preferences of each senior, allowing for tailored treatment plans that address their unique challenges. This personalized approach helps seniors feel heard, understood, and empowered on their recovery journey.
2. **Focus on overall well-being**: Holistic therapies emphasize not only the management of substance abuse but also the promotion of overall well-being. Through activities such as yoga, meditation, and nutritional guidance, seniors can improve their physical health, reduce stress, and enhance their emotional resilience.
3. **Integration of complementary therapies**: Holistic approaches often incorporate complementary therapies such as acupuncture, massage, and art therapy. These therapies can provide seniors with alternative ways to cope with stress, manage pain, and express themselves creatively, enhancing their overall treatment experience.

Promoting Holistic Healing and Wellness

Promoting holistic healing and wellness for seniors with substance abuse involves recognizing the mind-body connection and addressing it through alternative therapy options.

By incorporating practices such as yoga, meditation, and acupuncture, seniors can experience physical and mental healing that complements their traditional treatment.

Encouraging self-care practices, like engaging in hobbies, staying socially connected, and maintaining a healthy lifestyle, can also contribute to their overall well-being.

Mind-Body Connection

What is the crucial link between the mind and body when it comes to promoting holistic healing and wellness for seniors with substance abuse?

1. **Emotional well-being**: The mind-body connection plays a significant role in promoting emotional well-being for seniors with substance abuse. By addressing their emotional needs and providing support, we can help them develop healthier coping mechanisms and reduce the reliance on substances.
2. **Physical health**: Substance abuse takes a toll on the body, affecting overall physical health. By promoting holistic healing, we aim to improve seniors' physical well-being through proper nutrition, exercise, and medical care. This integrated approach helps restore their body's natural balance and vitality.
3. **Mental clarity**: Substance abuse often clouds the mind, leading to cognitive impairments and mental health issues. By emphasizing the mind-body connection, we can support seniors in achieving mental clarity through therapy, mindfulness practices, and cognitive exercises. These fosters improved decision-making, self-awareness, and a

sense of purpose in their recovery journey.

Understanding the crucial link between the mind and body allows us to provide comprehensive care that promotes holistic healing and wellness for seniors with substance abuse.

Alternative Therapy Options

Alternative therapy options offer seniors with substance abuse a diverse range of holistic healing and wellness approaches to support their recovery journey. These therapies focus on promoting overall well-being by addressing the physical, emotional, and spiritual aspects of a person.

One popular alternative therapy is acupuncture, which involves the insertion of thin needles into specific points on the body to restore balance and alleviate cravings.

Another option is mindfulness-based stress reduction (MBSR), which combines meditation, yoga, and other relaxation techniques to enhance self-awareness and reduce stress.

Art therapy and music therapy are also effective tools for self-expression and emotional healing.

Additionally, equine therapy, where seniors interact with horses, can help build trust, improve communication, and foster emotional growth.

Self-Care Practices

Incorporating self-care practices is essential in promoting holistic healing and wellness for seniors with substance abuse. Engaging in self-care activities can help seniors regain control of their lives and develop healthy coping mechanisms.

Here are three self-care practices that can have a profound impact on their well-being:

1. **Regular exercise**: Engaging in physical activities not only boosts physical health but also improves mood and reduces stress. Seniors can try low-impact exercises such as yoga, swimming, or walking to

improve their overall well-being.
2. **Mindfulness and meditation**: Encouraging seniors to practice mindfulness and meditation can help them develop a greater sense of self-awareness and promote emotional stability. These practices can also assist in managing cravings and reducing anxiety.
3. **Social connection**: Building and maintaining social connections is vital for seniors. Encouraging them to join support groups or engage in hobbies can provide a sense of belonging and support, reducing feelings of isolation and loneliness.

Frequently Asked Questions

What Are Some Common Signs and Symptoms of Substance Abuse in Seniors?

Common signs and symptoms of substance abuse in seniors include changes in mood or behavior, increased isolation, poor hygiene, unexplained physical injuries, memory loss, and neglecting responsibilities. Early detection and intervention are crucial for their well-being.

Are There Any Specific Risk Factors or Challenges That Make Seniors More Vulnerable to Substance Abuse?

Seniors face unique risk factors and challenges that make them more vulnerable to substance abuse. These factors include chronic pain, loneliness, loss of loved ones, retirement, and limited social support. Understanding these factors is crucial in creating a supportive environment for seniors.

How Can Family Members or Caregivers Effectively Communicate with Seniors About Their Substance Abuse Issues?

Effective communication with seniors about substance abuse issues can be achieved through empathetic and non-judgmental approaches. Providing a supportive and safe environment, actively listening, and offering resources and assistance can help facilitate open and honest conversations.

Are There Any Alternative Treatment Options or Interventions Specifically Designed for Seniors with Substance Abuse?

There are alternative treatment options and interventions specifically designed for seniors with substance abuse. These interventions focus on addressing the unique needs and challenges that seniors face in order to provide effective and tailored support for their recovery journey.

What Are Some Strategies or Resources Available to Help Seniors Maintain Their Sobriety After Completing Treatment?

There are several strategies and resources available to help seniors maintain their sobriety after completing treatment. These include ongoing therapy, support groups, sober living homes, relapse prevention plans, and continued access to medical and mental health services.

Conclusion

In conclusion, creating a supportive environment for seniors with substance abuse requires understanding their unique needs. This includes recognizing the specific challenges they may face due to their age and the impact of substance abuse on their physical and mental health.

Another important aspect is ensuring a safe and secure physical environment. This involves creating an environment where seniors feel safe from external threats and have access to appropriate security measures.

Fostering emotional support and connection is also crucial. Seniors with substance abuse may experience feelings of isolation and loneliness, so it is important to provide opportunities for social interaction and emotional support.

Additionally, providing accessible and age-appropriate treatment options is essential. Seniors may require specialized treatment approaches that take into account their physical health, cognitive abilities, and unique circumstances.

Finally, promoting holistic healing and wellness is important for seniors with substance abuse. This involves addressing their physical, emotional, and spiritual needs through various therapies and support services.

By addressing these aspects, we can empower seniors to overcome their substance abuse challenges and enhance their overall well-being. It is crucial to approach this issue with empathy, knowledge, and information to effectively support seniors in their journey towards recovery.

CHAPTER 4: TAILORED TREATMENT APPROACHES

In Chapter 4, we explore the crucial topic of tailored treatment approaches for seniors with substance abuse problems. As the aging population continues to grow, it becomes increasingly important to address the unique challenges faced by this demographic in their journey towards recovery. By understanding the factors contributing to senior substance abuse, implementing specialized treatment strategies, and creating an environment conducive to their recovery, we can make significant strides in improving the quality of life for seniors struggling with addiction.

Additionally, we will probe into the importance of sensitivity in senior substance abuse treatment, recognizing the need for personalized care that considers their specific needs and experiences. Through exploring these tailored treatment approaches, we hope to shed light on effective methods that can empower seniors to reclaim their lives and find lasting sobriety.

Key Takeaways

- Age-related risk factors, social isolation and loneliness, and co-occurring health conditions contribute to senior substance abuse.
- Tailored treatment approaches are crucial for effectively addressing substance abuse in seniors.

- Treatment strategies should consider age-related risk factors and the specific needs and concerns of older adults.
- Interventions that address social isolation and co-occurring health conditions should be incorporated into treatment approaches for seniors.

Factors Contributing to Senior Substance Abuse

When addressing the factors contributing to senior substance abuse, it is crucial to consider age-related risk factors, such as chronic pain or cognitive decline, which may lead to the misuse of prescription medications.

Additionally, social isolation and loneliness can play a significant role, as seniors may turn to substances as a coping mechanism for feelings of loneliness or boredom.

Moreover, co-occurring health conditions, such as depression or anxiety, can further complicate the issue, as seniors may use substances to self-medicate.

Understanding these factors is essential in developing tailored treatment approaches that address the unique needs of seniors struggling with substance abuse.

Age-Related Risk Factors

As individuals age, there are various risk factors that contribute to substance abuse among seniors, necessitating tailored treatment approaches that address these unique challenges.

Aging comes with a multitude of physical, emotional, and social changes that can increase vulnerability to substance abuse. Physical ailments, such as chronic pain or health conditions, may lead to the misuse of prescription medications.

Emotional factors, such as grief, loneliness, or depression, can drive individuals towards self-medication with alcohol or drugs. Social isolation, loss of social support systems, and retirement may also contribute to substance abuse among seniors.

Understanding these age-related risk factors is crucial for developing effective treatment strategies that consider the specific needs and concerns of older adults struggling with substance abuse.

Social Isolation and Loneliness

Seniors who experience social isolation and loneliness face an increased risk of substance abuse, highlighting the importance of addressing these factors in tailored treatment approaches.

As individuals age, they may experience various life changes that can lead to feelings of isolation and loneliness. Retirement, loss of loved ones, and declining health can all contribute to a reduced social network and a sense of disconnection from others. These feelings can be particularly challenging for seniors, as they may have limited opportunities for social interaction and support.

Substance abuse can become a coping mechanism for these individuals, providing temporary relief from their emotional pain. Therefore, it is crucial to incorporate interventions that address social isolation and loneliness into treatment plans for seniors with substance abuse issues.

Co-Occurring Health Conditions

Many older adults struggling with substance abuse also face concurrent health conditions that contribute to their addiction. These co-occurring health conditions can include physical ailments, such as chronic pain, arthritis, or mobility issues, as well as mental health disorders like depression, anxiety, or cognitive decline.

The relationship between these health conditions and substance abuse is complex and intertwined. For some seniors, the misuse of substances may initially be an attempt to self-medicate and alleviate the symptoms of their health conditions. However, over time, substance abuse can worsen these conditions and lead to a vicious cycle of dependency.

It is crucial for healthcare professionals to recognize and address these co-occurring health conditions when developing tailored treatment approaches for seniors with substance abuse. By addressing both the addiction and the underlying health conditions, individuals can receive comprehensive care that improves their overall well-being and increases their chances of successful recovery.

Specialized Treatment Strategies for Seniors

When it comes to treating substance abuse in seniors, it is important to consider their age-related health considerations. This includes understanding the impact of medications and physical health issues on their treatment.

Additionally, special attention should be given to cognitive impairment management to ensure that treatment strategies are tailored to their cognitive abilities.

Age-Related Health Considerations

As individuals age, it becomes increasingly important to consider their unique health considerations when developing specialized treatment strategies for substance abuse.

Aging brings about various changes in the body, including a decline in organ function, changes in metabolism, and an increased vulnerability to the adverse effects of substances. These age-related changes can affect the way seniors respond to substance abuse treatment, making it crucial to tailor interventions to their specific needs.

One important consideration is the impact of medications on substance abuse treatment. Many seniors take multiple medications for chronic health conditions, and these medications can interact with substances of abuse, potentially leading to adverse effects or reduced treatment efficacy. Additionally, seniors may have comorbid medical conditions, such as cardiovascular disease or diabetes, which require careful management during treatment.

Another crucial aspect is the potential for cognitive impairment in older adults. Substance abuse can exacerbate cognitive decline, making it essential to address both the substance abuse and cognitive issues in treatment. This may involve cognitive remediation strategies, memory aids, and modifications to treatment approaches to accommodate cognitive limitations.

Furthermore, seniors may experience greater physical frailty, which can impact their ability to participate in treatment activities or adhere to treatment plans. Adjustments may be necessary to ensure that treatment is accessible and feasible for seniors with physical limitations.

Lastly, mental health considerations are essential when treating seniors with substance abuse issues. Older adults may be more susceptible to depression, anxiety, and other mental health disorders, which can complicate substance abuse treatment. Integrated treatment approaches that address both substance abuse and mental health issues are crucial in promoting positive outcomes for seniors.

Cognitive Impairment Management

Tailoring treatment strategies for seniors with substance abuse requires a comprehensive approach that addresses the unique challenges posed by cognitive impairment. Cognitive impairment can impact an individual's ability to understand and engage in treatment, making it crucial to adapt treatment strategies to meet their specific needs.

To effectively manage cognitive impairment, treatment providers must have a deep understanding of the underlying causes and manifestations of cognitive decline in seniors. This knowledge allows for the development of specialized treatment plans that focus on enhancing cognitive function, promoting memory retention, and improving overall mental well-being.

Additionally, it is vital to create a supportive and compassionate environment that fosters trust and understanding. Treatment providers should employ strategies such as simplified explanations, visual aids, and repetition to facilitate comprehension and retention of information.

Social Support Networks

To further enhance tailored treatment strategies for seniors with substance abuse, it is crucial to address the importance of establishing robust social support networks that cater to their unique needs.

Seniors struggling with substance abuse often face isolation and loneliness, compounding their challenges. By creating a strong network of supportive relationships, we can provide the necessary empathy, encouragement, and guidance they need to navigate their recovery journey.

Social support networks can include family members, friends, support groups, and healthcare professionals who specialize in senior addiction treatment. These networks play a vital role in reducing the stigma associated with substance abuse among seniors and promoting a sense of belonging and understanding.

Through these networks, seniors can share experiences, gain insights, and develop coping mechanisms that are specific to their age-related concerns, fostering a sense of hope and motivation.

With the help of robust social support networks, seniors can find solace, encouragement, and the strength to overcome their substance abuse challenges.

Addressing Unique Challenges of Aging Population

As seniors face the unique challenges of aging, it is crucial to address the intersection of cognitive decline and addiction. Cognitive impairments can complicate treatment and recovery efforts, requiring tailored approaches that consider memory loss, decision-making difficulties, and limited insight into their substance abuse.

Additionally, physical health considerations must be considered, as aging bodies may be more vulnerable to the negative effects of substance abuse.

Lastly, social isolation can contribute to substance abuse among seniors, highlighting the importance of creating supportive networks and addressing the underlying causes of loneliness and isolation.

Cognitive Decline and Addiction

Seniors facing the unique challenges of cognitive decline and addiction require tailored treatment approaches that combine empathy, knowledge, and compassion. As we age, our cognitive abilities may diminish, making it even more difficult to recover from addiction. It is crucial to understand that cognitive decline can impact a senior's ability to comprehend and follow treatment plans effectively.

To address this issue, treatment programs should consider the following:

- **Provide cognitive assessments**: Conducting comprehensive assessments can help identify the extent of cognitive decline and tailor treatment accordingly.
- **Incorporate memory aids and reminders**: Use memory aids, such as calendars or medication organizers, to help seniors stay on track with their treatment plans.
- **Offer specialized therapy**: Cognitive behavioral therapy (CBT) and other evidence-based therapies can be adapted to accommodate cognitive challenges.

Physical Health Considerations

Addressing the unique challenges of the aging population, it is essential to consider physical health considerations when developing tailored treatment approaches for seniors facing cognitive decline and addiction.

Physical health plays a crucial role in the overall well-being of seniors, and it is important to address any underlying health issues that may impact their addiction recovery journey. As individuals age, they may experience a decline in physical functioning, chronic pain, and increased vulnerability to illness. These factors can complicate the treatment process and require specialized care.

It is crucial for healthcare professionals to conduct a comprehensive physical assessment to identify any physical health issues that may need attention. Integrating physical therapy, pain management strategies, and other appropriate interventions into the treatment plan can help seniors improve their physical health and enhance their chances of successful recovery.

Social Isolation and Substance Abuse

Social isolation can pose unique challenges for the aging population struggling with substance abuse. As individuals age, they may experience the loss of loved ones and a decrease in social interactions, leading to feelings of loneliness and isolation. This isolation can exacerbate substance abuse issues and hinder recovery efforts.

To address the specific needs of seniors facing social isolation and substance abuse, treatment approaches should consider the following:

- Encouraging participation in support groups or therapy sessions to foster a sense of community and provide emotional support.
- Promoting engagement in social activities and hobbies can help individuals build new relationships and combat loneliness.
- Providing transportation services or assisting with mobility challenges to enable seniors to attend social events and connect with others.

- Offering education and resources to help seniors strengthen their social support networks and develop healthier coping mechanisms.

Creating an Environment for Senior Recovery

Creating a safe and supportive environment is crucial in facilitating the recovery of seniors struggling with substance abuse. By providing individualized treatment plans that address the unique needs and challenges of each senior, we can increase the chances of successful outcomes.

Taking a holistic care approach, considering physical, mental, and emotional well-being, will help create an environment that promotes healing and empowers seniors to regain control of their lives.

Safe and Supportive

Seniors recovering from substance abuse require a nurturing and secure environment that promotes their well-being and aids in their healing journey. Creating a safe and supportive space is crucial for their recovery. Here are some key elements to consider:

Physical environment:

- Providing a clean and comfortable living space that is free from triggers and substances.
- Ensuring easy access to medical care and assistance for any health concerns.

Emotional support:

- Building a compassionate and non-judgmental atmosphere where seniors feel understood and valued.
- Offering individual and group therapy sessions to address emotional needs and foster a sense of community.

Individualized Treatment Plans

Tailored treatment plans are essential in creating an environment conducive to senior recovery, as they address the unique needs and circumstances of everyone. Seniors struggling with substance abuse require personalized treatment approaches that consider their physical health, cognitive abilities, and emotional well-being.

By developing individualized treatment plans, healthcare professionals can ensure that seniors receive the right level of care, support, and guidance throughout their recovery journey. These plans consider factors such as the type and severity of substance abuse, any co-occurring mental health conditions, and the presence of chronic medical conditions.

Additionally, they incorporate strategies to address the challenges specific to seniors, such as social isolation, loss of support systems, and age-related physical limitations.

Holistic Care Approach

To provide comprehensive care for seniors struggling with substance abuse, it is crucial to foster an environment that promotes their overall well-being and recovery. A holistic care approach addresses not only the physical aspects of addiction but also the mental, emotional, and social dimensions. By taking into account the unique needs and challenges faced by seniors, this approach ensures a personalized and targeted treatment plan.

To create an environment conducive to senior recovery, the following strategies can be implemented:

- **Integration of medical and mental health services**: By offering integrated care, seniors can receive both medical and mental health support in one place, reducing barriers to treatment and improving overall outcomes.
- **Emphasis on social support**: Encouraging seniors to engage in support groups and counseling sessions

- can provide valuable peer support and help combat feelings of isolation.
- **Incorporation of alternative therapies**: Complementary therapies such as yoga, meditation, and art therapy can help seniors develop healthy coping mechanisms and reduce stress.

Importance of Sensitivity in Senior Substance Abuse Treatment

When it comes to treating seniors with substance abuse, it is crucial to approach their treatment with sensitivity and understanding. Age-related physiological changes can impact the way medications are metabolized and how the body responds to treatment.

Additionally, seniors may face unique mental health challenges such as loneliness, grief, or cognitive decline, which require specialized care.

Lastly, considering the importance of social support in recovery, treatment approaches should involve family members, caregivers, and support networks to ensure a comprehensive and compassionate approach to their treatment.

Age-Related Physiological Changes

With advancing age, seniors experience a range of physiological changes that necessitate a sensitive approach when providing substance abuse treatment. It is crucial to understand and address these age-related changes to ensure the effectiveness of treatment interventions.

Here are some key considerations:

- **Metabolism and Drug Absorption**: Due to a decrease in liver and kidney function, seniors may metabolize drugs more slowly, leading to prolonged drug effects and increased risk of toxicity. Adjustments in medication dosage and monitoring are essential.

- **Decline in Cognitive Function**: Age-related cognitive decline can affect a senior's ability to comprehend and engage in treatment. Tailoring interventions to accommodate cognitive impairments, such as providing simplified instructions or using visual aids, can enhance treatment outcomes.

Unique Mental Health Challenges

Seniors grappling with substance abuse face unique mental health challenges that demand a sensitive and compassionate approach to treatment.

As individuals age, they experience various life changes that can contribute to the development or exacerbation of mental health issues. These challenges include grief and loss, social isolation, loneliness, and physical health problems.

Additionally, older adults may have a higher prevalence of co-occurring mental health disorders, such as depression or anxiety, which can complicate their substance abuse treatment.

It is crucial for healthcare professionals to approach these individuals with empathy, knowledge, and compassion. By acknowledging and addressing their unique mental health challenges, treatment providers can help seniors on their path to recovery.

Tailored treatment plans that integrate mental health support and substance abuse treatment are essential in promoting successful outcomes and improving the overall well-being of older adults struggling with substance abuse.

Social Support Considerations

As healthcare professionals strive to provide effective treatment for seniors grappling with substance abuse, it is essential to consider the importance of social support and approach their unique needs with sensitivity and compassion. Seniors facing substance abuse issues often experience feelings of isolation and loneliness, making social support a crucial aspect of their recovery journey.

Here are two key considerations for healthcare professionals in providing social support for seniors with substance abuse:

Building a Supportive Network:
- Encourage involvement in support groups tailored for seniors, where they can connect with others facing similar challenges.
- Foster relationships with family members, friends, and caregivers to create a dedicated support system that can provide emotional and practical assistance.

Addressing Stigma and Shame:
- Create a non-judgmental and safe environment where seniors feel comfortable discussing their substance abuse issues.
- Educate the community and healthcare providers about the unique challenges faced by seniors with substance abuse, reducing stigma and facilitating understanding.

Frequently Asked Questions

How Can Family Members and Loved Ones of Seniors with Substance Abuse Issues Support Them During Their Recovery Journey?

Family members and loved ones of seniors with substance abuse issues can provide crucial support during their recovery journey by offering understanding, empathy, and encouragement. This can be done through active listening, attending therapy sessions, and participating in support groups together.

Are There Any Specific Medications or Treatment Options That Are Recommended for Seniors with Substance Abuse Problems?

There are specific medications and treatment options recommended for seniors with substance abuse problems.

These options can include medication-assisted therapy, counseling, support groups, and tailored treatment approaches that address the unique needs and challenges faced by older adults in recovery.

What Are Some Common Signs and Symptoms of Substance Abuse in Older Adults That Family Members Should Look Out For?

Family members should be aware of common signs and symptoms of substance abuse in older adults, including changes in behavior, mood swings, social withdrawal, neglecting personal hygiene, unexplained financial difficulties, and frequent health issues.

How Can Healthcare Professionals and Addiction Specialists Effectively Assess and Diagnose Substance Abuse in Seniors?

Healthcare professionals and addiction specialists can effectively assess and diagnose substance abuse in seniors through a comprehensive evaluation that includes medical history, physical examination, laboratory tests, and psychological assessments. This holistic approach allows for tailored treatment plans and improved outcomes.

Are There Any Specific Support Groups or Resources Available for Seniors with Substance Abuse Issues and Their Families?

Yes, there are specific support groups and resources available for seniors with substance abuse issues and their families. These include specialized addiction treatment centers, counseling services, and community-based organizations that offer support and guidance.

Conclusion

In conclusion, tailored treatment approaches for seniors with substance abuse are crucial in addressing the unique challenges faced by the aging population.

By considering factors contributing to senior substance abuse and implementing specialized treatment strategies, a supportive environment can be created to promote senior recovery.

Sensitivity and compassion play significant roles in senior substance abuse treatment, emphasizing the importance of understanding and empathizing with the specific needs and experiences of this population.

CHAPTER 5: DEVELOPING HEALTHY COPING MECHANISMS

Substance abuse among seniors is a complex issue that requires a comprehensive approach. In Chapter 5, we dig into the development of healthy coping mechanisms specifically tailored for this demographic.

By understanding the impact of substance abuse on seniors and identifying unhealthy coping mechanisms, we can begin to promote self-care and emotional well-being.

Additionally, encouraging supportive relationships and community involvement plays a crucial role in their journey towards recovery.

Join us as we explore the effective treatment and recovery strategies that can offer hope and a better quality of life for seniors struggling with substance abuse.

Key Takeaways

- Substance abuse has a significant impact on the health and well-being of seniors, leading to organ damage, cognitive decline, social isolation, and worsening mental and emotional health.
- Seniors with substance abuse face unique health risks and vulnerabilities, including drug interactions

and complications with multiple medications.
- Unhealthy coping mechanisms, such as increased isolation, neglecting personal hygiene, and self-destructive behaviors, can worsen seniors' overall well-being and contribute to substance abuse.
- Treatment options and support for seniors with substance abuse include inpatient rehabilitation programs, outpatient counseling, support groups, medication-assisted treatment, and individual therapy. Additionally, mindfulness, exercise, and social support are crucial healthy coping mechanisms for seniors in recovery.

Understanding the Impact of Substance Abuse on Seniors

Substance abuse among seniors can have a significant impact on their health and well-being. Seniors are more vulnerable to the health risks associated with substance abuse, such as organ damage and cognitive decline.

Additionally, substance abuse can contribute to social isolation and loneliness, further exacerbating the negative effects on their mental and emotional health.

It is crucial to understand these impacts in order to provide appropriate treatment options and support for seniors struggling with substance abuse.

Health Risks and Vulnerabilities

As individuals age, they face unique health risks and vulnerabilities that can be further exacerbated by the impact of substance abuse. It is important to understand the specific challenges that seniors with substance abuse face in order to provide effective support and treatment.

One of the main health risks for seniors with substance abuse is the potential for drug interactions and complications with multiple medications they may be taking for various health conditions. Additionally, substance abuse can worsen existing health conditions such as heart disease, diabetes, and respiratory problems.

Seniors may also experience cognitive decline and memory loss because of substance abuse. It is crucial to approach these health risks and vulnerabilities with empathy and knowledge, providing seniors with the necessary resources and assistance to address their substance abuse and improve their overall well-being.

Social Isolation and Loneliness

Seniors with substance abuse not only face unique health risks and vulnerabilities, but they also grapple with the profound impact of social isolation and loneliness on their well-being. Substance abuse can lead to strained relationships, loss of social connections, and isolation from loved ones. This isolation can exacerbate feelings of loneliness and despair, further fueling the cycle of substance abuse.

It is important to understand that social isolation and loneliness can significantly impact a senior's mental health, making recovery even more challenging. Recognizing the importance of social support, it is crucial to provide seniors with opportunities to rebuild and strengthen their social networks. This can be achieved through support groups, therapy, and community programs that promote social engagement.

Treatment Options and Support

Treatment options and support are essential components in addressing the impact of substance abuse on older adults. It is crucial to provide comprehensive care that focuses on both physical and mental well-being.

Here are some treatment options and support services available for seniors struggling with substance abuse:

- **Inpatient rehabilitation programs**: These programs provide 24/7 medical supervision and intensive

therapy to help seniors detox and develop healthier coping mechanisms.
- **Outpatient counseling**: This option allows seniors to receive treatment while still maintaining their daily routines and responsibilities.
- **Support groups**: Joining support groups can provide seniors with a sense of community and understanding, allowing them to share experiences and receive encouragement from others facing similar challenges.
- **Medication-assisted treatment**: Some seniors may benefit from medications that can help reduce cravings and manage withdrawal symptoms.
- **Individual therapy**: Working one-on-one with a therapist can help seniors explore the underlying causes of their substance abuse and develop personalized coping strategies.

Identifying Unhealthy Coping Mechanisms in Seniors

As we explore the topic of developing healthy coping mechanisms for seniors with substance abuse, it is crucial to first identify the unhealthy coping mechanisms they may be employing. Warning signs such as increased isolation, neglecting personal hygiene, or changes in mood and behavior can indicate the presence of unhealthy coping strategies.

Common self-destructive behaviors, such as substance abuse, self-harm, or excessive gambling, can further exacerbate the negative impact on their overall well-being. Recognizing these signs and behaviors is the first step in providing the necessary support and intervention for seniors struggling with substance abuse.

Warning Signs of Unhealthy Coping

Identifying signs of unhealthy coping mechanisms is crucial when addressing the unique challenges that seniors face in dealing with substance abuse. It is important to recognize these warning signs to intervene and provide the necessary support and treatment for seniors.

Here are some key indicators that may suggest unhealthy coping mechanisms:

- **Increased isolation**: Seniors who withdraw from social activities and relationships may be using substances to cope with their emotions or difficulties.
- **Neglected physical appearance**: Lack of personal grooming and hygiene can be a sign that seniors are prioritizing substance use over self-care.
- **Sudden changes in mood or behavior**: Unexplained irritability, aggression, or depression may be indicative of substance abuse and unhealthy coping mechanisms.
- **Neglected responsibilities**: Seniors who neglect their daily responsibilities, such as paying bills or maintaining their home, may struggle with substance abuse.
- **Financial difficulties**: A sudden decline in financial stability, frequent requests for money, or unexplained expenses can be a red flag for substance abuse.

Common Self-Destructive Behaviors

When it comes to addressing the unique challenges that seniors face in dealing with substance abuse, it is crucial to identify common self-destructive behaviors that may indicate unhealthy coping mechanisms.

Seniors who struggle with substance abuse may engage in various self-destructive behaviors as a way to cope with their emotions and the challenges they face. These behaviors can include isolating themselves from loved ones, neglecting personal hygiene and self-care, experiencing changes in sleep patterns, appetite, and weight, exhibiting frequent mood swings or irritability, and engaging in risky behaviors such as driving under the influence or sharing needles.

It is important to approach seniors with empathy and understanding, as these behaviors are often a symptom of deeper emotional pain. By recognizing these behaviors, we can provide the necessary support and guidance to help seniors develop healthier coping mechanisms and overcome substance abuse.

Negative Impact on Well-Being

Seniors grappling with substance abuse may unknowingly resort to detrimental coping mechanisms that significantly impact their overall well-being. It is important to identify these unhealthy coping mechanisms to address them effectively.

Here are some common negative impacts on well-being that seniors may experience:

- **Physical health deterioration**: Substance abuse can lead to a decline in physical health, causing issues such as chronic pain, weakened immune system, and increased risk of diseases.
- **Mental health challenges**: Seniors may develop or exacerbate mental health conditions like anxiety, depression, or cognitive impairment.
- **Social isolation**: Substance abuse can lead to withdrawal from social activities and relationships, resulting in feelings of loneliness and isolation.
- **Financial instability**: Seniors may experience financial difficulties due to the cost of the substances, leading to stress on their finances.
- **Decline in overall quality of life**: Unhealthy coping mechanisms can negatively impact seniors' ability to enjoy life, pursue meaningful activities, and maintain a sense of purpose.

Understanding the negative impact of these coping mechanisms is crucial in order to develop healthier alternatives that promote well-being and recovery.

Promoting Self-Care and Emotional Well-being

Promoting self-care and emotional well-being is crucial for seniors with substance abuse issues.

Mindfulness and meditation can help seniors develop a greater sense of self-awareness and manage stress and cravings.

Engaging in regular exercise and physical activity not only improves physical health but also boosts mood and cognitive function.

Lastly, having a strong social support network can provide seniors with the emotional support and encouragement they need on their journey towards recovery.

Mindfulness and Meditation

Mindfulness and meditation are powerful tools for fostering self-care and emotional well-being among seniors struggling with substance abuse. These practices can help seniors cultivate a greater sense of awareness and presence, allowing them to better manage their cravings, emotions, and stress.

Here are some key benefits of incorporating mindfulness and meditation into their recovery journey:

- Promotes relaxation and stress reduction, providing seniors with a healthy outlet for managing anxiety and tension.
- Enhances self-awareness, helping seniors recognize triggers and negative thought patterns that contribute to substance abuse.
- Cultivates acceptance and non-judgment, allowing seniors to let go of self-blame and develop a compassionate attitude towards themselves.
- Improves mental clarity and focus, enabling seniors

- to make more conscious and informed decisions.
- Supports emotional regulation, empowering seniors to navigate challenging emotions in a healthy and constructive manner.

Exercise and Physical Activity

Incorporating regular exercise and physical activity into the daily routine can contribute to the self-care and emotional well-being of seniors struggling with substance abuse.

Engaging in physical activity not only improves physical health but also has a positive impact on mental and emotional well-being. Exercise releases endorphins, the body's natural mood-enhancing chemicals, which can help alleviate symptoms of anxiety and depression commonly associated with substance abuse.

Moreover, physical activity provides a healthy outlet for stress, reducing the likelihood of relapse. Seniors can benefit from various forms of exercise, such as walking, swimming, or yoga, tailored to their abilities and preferences.

Encouraging seniors to incorporate exercise into their daily routine can promote a sense of empowerment, improve self-esteem, and contribute to overall recovery and well-being.

Social Support Network

Establishing a strong social support network is essential for promoting self-care and emotional well-being in seniors struggling with substance abuse. Seniors dealing with addiction often face feelings of isolation, shame, and guilt, making it crucial to build a network of supportive individuals who can provide understanding, encouragement, and guidance.

Here are some ways a social support network can help seniors in their journey towards recovery:

- **Emotional support**: Having someone to talk to and share their feelings with can alleviate the emotional

burden and provide a sense of validation.
- **Accountability**: A support network can hold seniors accountable for their actions and help them stay on track with their recovery goals.
- **Practical assistance**: Friends and family can offer practical help such as accompanying seniors to therapy sessions or providing transportation for support group meetings.
- **Peer connection**: Connecting with others who have experienced similar struggles can provide a sense of belonging and inspire hope.
- **Social activities**: Engaging in social activities with supportive friends can help seniors build new, healthier relationships and reduce the desire to use substances.

Encouraging Supportive Relationships and Community Involvement

Building supportive relationships and fostering community involvement are crucial for seniors with substance abuse issues.

Social engagement benefits their overall well-being by providing a sense of connection, reducing feelings of isolation, and enhancing their support network.

It is important to highlight the various community resources available that can facilitate these relationships and encourage seniors to actively participate in activities that promote social interaction and a sense of belonging.

Social Engagement Benefits

Encouraging seniors to cultivate supportive relationships and actively participate in their communities can enhance their overall well-being and resilience in overcoming substance abuse challenges. Social engagement offers numerous benefits that can help seniors on their journey to recovery.

Here are some ways in which social engagement can positively impact seniors with substance abuse:

- **Emotional support**: Having supportive relationships can provide seniors with a sense of belonging, validation, and understanding, which can boost their emotional well-being.
- **Accountability**: Being engaged in a community can help seniors stay accountable for their actions and decisions, as they are surrounded by individuals who care about their recovery.
- **Distraction and fulfillment**: Participating in community activities can provide seniors with a sense of purpose, fulfillment, and diversion from substance abuse cravings.
- **Learning and growth**: Engaging with others allows seniors to learn new skills, gain knowledge, and develop new interests, contributing to personal growth.
- **Reduced isolation**: Social engagement can alleviate feelings of loneliness and isolation, creating a supportive network that reduces the risk of relapse.

Importance of Connections

Creating and nurturing supportive relationships and actively participating in community involvement are crucial for seniors with substance abuse as they embark on the path to recovery.

The importance of connections cannot be overstated in the recovery process, as they provide a sense of belonging, support, and accountability. Supportive relationships can provide emotional support, encouragement, and understanding, helping seniors navigate the challenges of substance abuse recovery. These connections can also serve as a valuable source of guidance and advice, offering practical strategies for maintaining sobriety and preventing relapse.

Additionally, community involvement can provide seniors with a sense of purpose and fulfillment, helping them rebuild their lives after addiction. By actively engaging in community activities, seniors can establish new connections, expand their social network, and find meaningful ways to contribute to the community.

Ultimately, fostering supportive relationships and participating in community involvement can significantly enhance the recovery journey for seniors with substance abuse.

Community Resources Available

To support seniors with substance abuse in fostering strong connections and active community involvement, a range of valuable community resources are available to provide support, guidance, and opportunities for growth. These resources can play a crucial role in helping seniors overcome their addiction and lead healthier, more fulfilling lives.

Some of the community resources available include:

- **Support groups**: These groups offer a safe and understanding environment where seniors can share their experiences, receive emotional support, and learn from others who have faced similar challenges.
- **Counseling services**: Professional counselors can provide seniors with the individualized support they need, helping them address underlying issues and develop effective coping strategies.
- **Treatment centers**: These facilities offer specialized programs and therapies tailored to the unique needs of seniors, providing them with comprehensive care and helping them on their path to recovery.
- **Community outreach programs**: These programs aim to raise awareness about substance abuse among seniors and provide education and resources to both seniors and their families.
- **Volunteer opportunities**: Engaging in volunteer work not only helps seniors give back to their community but also provides them with a sense of

purpose and connection, reducing the risk of relapse.

Implementing Effective Treatment and Recovery Strategies

Implementing effective treatment and recovery strategies is crucial in helping seniors with substance abuse overcome their addiction and regain their health and well-being.

One important aspect of this is providing therapy options that are specifically tailored to the needs of seniors, considering their unique physical and emotional challenges.

Additionally, supportive community programs can play a vital role in providing a sense of belonging and encouragement throughout the recovery process.

Taking a holistic approach that addresses both the physical and mental aspects of addiction can increase the chances of successful recovery for seniors.

Therapy Options for Seniors

Seniors struggling with substance abuse can benefit from a range of therapy options that focus on implementing effective treatment and recovery strategies. Therapy provides a safe and supportive environment for seniors to address their addiction, learn healthy coping mechanisms, and work towards long-term recovery.

Here are five therapy options that can be particularly helpful for seniors:

- **Individual therapy**: One-on-one sessions with a therapist can help seniors explore the underlying causes of their substance abuse, develop personalized strategies for recovery, and gain insight into their emotions and behaviors.
- **Group therapy**: Participating in group sessions allows seniors to connect with others who are facing similar challenges, share experiences, and receive

support and encouragement from peers.
- **Cognitive-behavioral therapy (CBT)**: This approach helps seniors identify and change negative thought patterns and behaviors that contribute to substance abuse.
- **Family therapy**: Involving family members in therapy sessions can help seniors rebuild relationships, address family dynamics and conflicts, and strengthen their support system.
- **Holistic therapy**: Incorporating complementary therapies like yoga, meditation, art therapy, or music therapy can enhance seniors' overall well-being and provide alternative ways to cope with stress and cravings.

These therapy options, when tailored to the specific needs of seniors, can empower them to overcome substance abuse, achieve recovery, and lead fulfilling lives.

Supportive Community Programs

Supportive community programs play a crucial role in implementing effective treatment and recovery strategies for seniors struggling with substance abuse. These programs provide a safe and understanding environment where seniors can connect with others who are going through similar experiences.

By offering a sense of belonging and support, community programs help seniors build a network of individuals who can uplift and guide them on their recovery journey. These programs often include group therapy sessions, educational workshops, and recreational activities that promote healthy coping mechanisms. They also offer access to specialized professionals who can provide personalized care and guidance.

Additionally, community programs help seniors develop new skills and interests, fostering a sense of purpose and fulfillment. With the support and encouragement from a community, seniors can find solace, strength, and the motivation needed to overcome substance abuse and live a healthier, happier life.

Holistic Approach to Recovery

As seniors engage in supportive community programs, they can further enhance their recovery journey by embracing a holistic approach to treatment and implementing effective strategies for long-term healing. A holistic approach recognizes that substance abuse affects the mind, body, and spirit, and seeks to address these interconnected aspects of a person's well-being. By adopting a holistic approach, seniors can experience comprehensive healing and find sustainable recovery.

Here are five key components of a holistic approach to recovery:

- **Physical well-being**: Incorporating regular exercise, nutritious diet, and adequate rest to promote overall health and vitality.
- **Emotional support**: Engaging in therapy, support groups, and counseling to address underlying emotional issues and develop healthy coping mechanisms.
- **Spiritual growth**: Exploring personal beliefs, finding meaning and purpose, and connecting with a higher power or inner self.
- **Mindfulness and meditation**: Cultivating present moment awareness, reducing stress, and improving self-awareness.
- **Complementary therapies**: Exploring alternative therapies such as acupuncture, yoga, and art therapy to promote relaxation, self-expression, and inner healing.

Frequently Asked Questions

What Are Some Common Signs and Symptoms of Substance Abuse in Seniors?

Some common signs and symptoms of substance abuse

in seniors include changes in behavior, mood swings, neglecting personal hygiene, withdrawal from social activities, unexplained financial problems, and physical health issues. It is important to address these concerns with empathy and support.

How Can Family Members and Loved Ones Support Seniors in Developing Healthy Coping Mechanisms?

Family members and loved ones can support seniors in developing healthy coping mechanisms by providing emotional support, encouraging participation in therapy or support groups, helping to create a supportive and nurturing environment, and promoting engagement in positive activities and hobbies.

Are There Any Specific Challenges That Seniors Face When It Comes to Overcoming Substance Abuse?

Seniors face unique challenges when overcoming substance abuse. These may include physical health issues, social isolation, and a lack of support networks. It is crucial to provide them with targeted interventions and resources to address these specific challenges.

What Are Some Alternative Therapies or Interventions That Can Be Effective in Treating Substance Abuse in Seniors?

Alternative therapies and interventions can be effective in treating substance abuse in seniors. These include cognitive-behavioral therapy, motivational interviewing, group therapy, and mindfulness-based stress reduction. These approaches address underlying issues and provide support for healthy coping mechanisms.

How Can Healthcare Professionals Play a Role in Identifying and Addressing Substance Abuse in Seniors?

Healthcare professionals play a crucial role in identifying and addressing substance abuse in seniors by conducting screenings, providing education, offering counseling and therapy, coordinating care with other providers, and supporting the implementation of healthy coping mechanisms.

Conclusion

In conclusion, it is crucial to develop healthy coping mechanisms for seniors with substance abuse.

By understanding the impact of substance abuse on seniors and identifying unhealthy coping mechanisms, we can promote their self-care and emotional well-being.

Encouraging supportive relationships and community involvement also play a vital role in their recovery process.

By implementing effective treatment and recovery strategies, we can support seniors in overcoming substance abuse and living a healthier and happier life.

CHAPTER 6: ADDRESSING CO-OCCURRING HEALTH ISSUES

In an aging population that is increasingly affected by substance abuse, it is crucial to address the co-occurring health issues that seniors face.

Chapter 6 provides valuable insights into the complex relationship between substance abuse and physical and mental health challenges in older adults.

By exploring the impact of substance abuse on physical well-being and the unique mental health struggles seniors may encounter, this chapter sheds light on the importance of effective interventions for their recovery.

As we dive into the intricacies of this topic, we will uncover the strategies and approaches that can make a significant difference in the lives of seniors struggling with substance abuse and co-occurring health issues.

Key Takeaways

- Co-occurring health issues in seniors with substance abuse can complicate the recovery process.
- Integrated care that addresses both substance abuse and co-occurring conditions is necessary.

- Co-occurring health issues can lead to increased healthcare utilization, hospitalizations, and relapse.
- Treating co-occurring health issues holistically can improve the overall well-being of seniors with substance abuse.

Growing Prevalence of Senior Substance Abuse

The prevalence of substance abuse among seniors is on the rise, necessitating a closer examination of this concerning trend. Senior substance abuse refers to the misuse or excessive use of alcohol, prescription medications, or illicit drugs by individuals aged 65 and older. This demographic is particularly vulnerable due to factors such as increased access to medications, retirement-related stressors, and the presence of age-related health conditions.

According to recent studies, the prevalence of substance abuse among seniors has been steadily increasing. This can be attributed to several factors, including the aging baby boomer population, the normalization of substance use in older adults, and the lack of awareness and screening for substance abuse in this age group. Additionally, the use of multiple medications by seniors, commonly known as polypharmacy, can increase the risk of substance abuse and addiction.

The consequences of senior substance abuse can have a significant impact on both physical and mental health. Older adults may experience adverse drug interactions, falls, cognitive impairment, and an increased risk of developing chronic diseases. Furthermore, substance abuse can exacerbate symptoms of depression, anxiety, and other mental health conditions commonly experienced by seniors.

Addressing the growing prevalence of substance abuse among seniors requires a comprehensive approach. This includes increasing awareness, implementing screening protocols, providing education on the risks of substance abuse, and offering effective treatment options tailored to the unique needs of older adults. By addressing this issue proactively, healthcare professionals can help mitigate the negative consequences associated with senior substance abuse and improve the overall well-being of this vulnerable population.

Understanding Co-Occurring Health Issues

Understanding the co-occurring health issues in seniors with substance abuse is crucial in developing effective treatment strategies. Risk factors such as chronic medical conditions, mental health disorders, and cognitive decline can complicate the recovery process.

Additionally, the impact of these health issues on treatment outcomes highlights the need for an integrated care approach that addresses both substance abuse and co-occurring conditions simultaneously.

Risk Factors for Seniors

Seniors with substance abuse face a range of risk factors that contribute to the development of co-occurring health issues. It is important to understand these risk factors to provide effective care and support for this vulnerable population.

The following are some of the key risk factors for seniors with substance abuse:

- **Chronic health conditions**: Seniors who have pre-existing chronic health conditions such as heart disease, diabetes, or arthritis are at a higher risk of developing co-occurring health issues when they engage in substance abuse.
- **Social isolation**: Seniors who are socially isolated, lacking social support, or experiencing loneliness are more likely to turn to substance abuse as a coping mechanism, increasing their risk of co-occurring health issues.
- **Medication interactions**: Seniors often take multiple medications, which can interact with substances and

exacerbate health issues.

These risk factors highlight the complex interplay between substance abuse and health issues in seniors. By addressing these risk factors, healthcare providers can improve outcomes and quality of life for this population.

Impact on Treatment Outcomes

Effective treatment outcomes for seniors with co-occurring health issues require a comprehensive understanding of the impact of these health issues on their recovery journey.

The presence of co-occurring health issues can significantly complicate the treatment process, making it essential to address these issues in a holistic manner.

When seniors struggle with both substance abuse and other health conditions, such as diabetes or cardiovascular disease, their recovery may be hindered by factors such as medication interactions, physical limitations, and cognitive impairments.

These co-occurring health issues can also contribute to increased healthcare utilization, hospitalizations, and a higher risk of relapse.

Therefore, treatment programs need to adopt integrated approaches that address both substance abuse and health issues simultaneously to optimize treatment outcomes for seniors.

Integrated Care Approach

The successful implementation of an integrated care approach is crucial for addressing the complex nature of co-occurring health issues in seniors with substance abuse. This approach involves bringing together multiple healthcare professionals from various disciplines to collaboratively manage the physical, mental, and social health needs of individuals.

Here are three key components of an integrated care approach:

- **Comprehensive Assessment**: A thorough evaluation is conducted to identify all co-occurring health

issues, including substance abuse, mental health conditions, and physical ailments. This assessment helps in developing a personalized treatment plan that addresses all aspects of an individual's well-being.
- **Coordinated Care**: Healthcare providers work together to deliver coordinated and consistent care. This involves sharing information, coordinating appointments, and ensuring seamless transitions between different healthcare settings.
- **Multidisciplinary Team**: An integrated care team consists of professionals from various fields such as medicine, psychiatry, psychology, social work, and addiction counseling. This diverse team brings together expertise from different domains to provide holistic care.

Impact of Substance Abuse on Physical Health

Substance abuse can have serious health risks, particularly in older adults. The physical effects of addiction can lead to a range of health problems, including cardiovascular issues, liver disease, and respiratory problems.

Additionally, substance abuse can worsen or complicate chronic conditions such as diabetes, hypertension, and arthritis.

Health Risks of Substance Abuse

Substance abuse can have severe detrimental effects on the physical health of individuals. The impact of substance abuse on physical health is significant and can lead to a multitude of health risks.

- Substance abuse can increase the risk of developing chronic diseases such as cardiovascular disease, liver disease, and respiratory problems.
- It can weaken the immune system, making individuals more susceptible to infections and

illnesses.
- Substance abuse can also cause nutritional deficiencies, leading to weight loss, malnourishment, and weakened bones.

These health risks can have long-lasting consequences on the overall well-being of individuals.

It is crucial to address substance abuse and its impact on physical health to ensure the best possible outcomes for individuals struggling with addiction. By addressing these health risks, healthcare professionals can provide comprehensive care and support to those in need.

Physical Effects of Addiction

Given the significant impact substance abuse has on physical health, it is crucial to understand the specific physical effects of addiction. Substance abuse can lead to a wide range of physical health issues.

One of the most common effects is damage to vital organs such as the liver, heart, and lungs. Prolonged substance abuse can also weaken the immune system, making individuals more susceptible to infections and diseases. Additionally, substance abuse can cause nutritional deficiencies, leading to weight loss, muscle wasting, and weakened bones.

Physical effects may vary depending on the type of substance abused, the duration of abuse, and the individual's overall health. It is important to address these physical effects to provide comprehensive care for seniors with substance abuse issues.

Substance Abuse and Chronic Conditions

The impact of substance abuse on physical health extends beyond immediate physical effects, often leading to the development or exacerbation of chronic conditions. Substance abuse can have long-term consequences on the body, affecting various systems and organs.

Here are some ways substance abuse can impact physical health:

- Increased risk of cardiovascular diseases, such as heart attacks and strokes
- Damage to the liver, leading to conditions like cirrhosis and hepatitis.
- Weakening of the immune system, making individuals more susceptible to infections and diseases

Substance abuse can also worsen existing chronic conditions, such as diabetes, respiratory disorders, and mental health conditions. It is important to address substance abuse in seniors with co-occurring chronic conditions, as treating both issues simultaneously can improve overall health outcomes and quality of life.

Mental Health Challenges and Substance Abuse

Seniors struggling with substance abuse often face mental health challenges in addition to their addiction. Dual diagnosis treatment, which addresses both the substance abuse and the underlying mental health condition, is essential for effective recovery.

An integrated care approach that combines therapy, medication management, and support services can provide seniors with the comprehensive treatment they need to address their co-occurring disorders.

Dual Diagnosis Treatment

Addressing the complex interplay between mental health challenges and substance abuse is a crucial aspect of effective dual diagnosis treatment. When it comes to addressing the co-occurrence of mental health and substance abuse issues, a comprehensive approach is necessary.

Here are three important components of dual diagnosis treatment:

- **Integrated treatment**: This approach involves addressing both mental health and substance abuse simultaneously, as they are often interconnected. Integrated treatment programs may include therapy, medication management, and support groups.
- **Individualized care**: Each person's dual diagnosis is unique, so personalized treatment plans are essential. This may involve tailoring interventions to address specific mental health disorders and substance abuse patterns.
- **Recovery support**: Ongoing support is crucial for individuals with dual diagnosis. This can include aftercare programs, relapse prevention strategies, and access to community resources.

Co-Occurring Disorders

As individuals with dual diagnosis receive integrated treatment and personalized care, it is important to address the co-occurring disorders of mental health challenges and substance abuse.

Co-occurring disorders refer to the simultaneous presence of both a mental health condition and a substance abuse disorder. These conditions can often interact and exacerbate each other, making it crucial to treat them simultaneously.

Research has shown that individuals with co-occurring disorders have poorer treatment outcomes and are at a higher risk of relapse. Therefore, a comprehensive approach that addresses both mental health challenges and substance abuse is essential for effective treatment.

This may involve a combination of medication, therapy, and support groups to address both the underlying mental health condition and the substance abuse disorder.

Integrated Care Approach

A comprehensive approach to treatment that addresses both

mental health challenges and substance abuse is crucial for individuals with co-occurring disorders. An integrated care approach offers a holistic and collaborative approach to treating both mental health and substance use disorders simultaneously. This approach recognizes that these conditions often interact and influence each other, and therefore require a coordinated and integrated treatment plan.

Here are three key elements of an integrated care approach:

- **Collaboration between mental health and substance abuse providers**: This ensures that both aspects of the individual's condition are addressed and that treatment plans are coordinated.
- **Dual diagnosis treatment**: This specialized treatment approach focuses on addressing both mental health and substance use disorders concurrently, using evidence-based therapies and medications.
- **Holistic care**: Integrated care emphasizes addressing the individual's physical, emotional, and social needs, recognizing that these factors can impact their overall well-being and recovery.

Effective Interventions for Seniors' Recovery

There are several effective interventions that can support seniors in their recovery from substance abuse.

Therapeutic approaches, such as cognitive-behavioral therapy or motivational interviewing, can help seniors address the underlying issues contributing to their substance abuse.

Supportive community resources, such as 12-step programs or senior-specific support groups, can provide seniors with a sense of connection and encouragement in their recovery journey.

Additionally, holistic treatment options that consider the physical, mental, and emotional well-being of seniors can help promote long-term recovery and overall wellness.

Therapeutic Approaches for Seniors

Effective therapeutic approaches are crucial for promoting seniors' recovery from substance abuse and addressing their co-occurring health issues. Here are three therapeutic approaches that have shown success in helping seniors overcome substance abuse:

- **Cognitive-Behavioral Therapy (CBT)**: This approach helps seniors identify and change negative thought patterns and behaviors associated with substance abuse. CBT equips them with coping strategies to manage cravings, stress, and triggers.
- **Motivational Interviewing (MI)**: MI is a person-centered approach that focuses on enhancing seniors' motivation to change. By exploring their intrinsic motivations and values, therapists can help seniors build confidence and commitment to recovery.
- **Medication-Assisted Treatment (MAT)**: MAT combines medication with counseling and behavioral therapies to address substance abuse. Medications such as buprenorphine or naltrexone can help seniors manage withdrawal symptoms and cravings, while therapy provides the necessary support and guidance.

Supportive Community Resources

To further support seniors in their recovery from substance abuse, accessing supportive community resources is essential.

These resources provide crucial assistance and guidance to seniors as they navigate the challenges of overcoming addiction. Supportive community resources offer a range of services, including counseling, support groups, and educational programs.

These resources can help seniors address the underlying

causes of their substance abuse, develop coping mechanisms, and establish healthier lifestyles. Support groups offer seniors the opportunity to connect with others who share similar experiences, providing a sense of understanding, empathy, and encouragement.

Additionally, community resources often collaborate with healthcare professionals to ensure a comprehensive approach to seniors' recovery.

Holistic Treatment Options

Seniors seeking recovery from substance abuse can benefit from holistic treatment options that address their physical, mental, and emotional well-being. Holistic treatment takes into account the whole person, focusing on their mind, body, and spirit. It recognizes that substance abuse is often a symptom of underlying issues and aims to treat the root causes rather than just the addiction.

Some effective holistic treatment options for seniors include:

- **Integrative therapies**: These can include acupuncture, massage therapy, and yoga, which help reduce stress, improve physical health, and promote relaxation.
- **Cognitive-behavioral therapy**: This form of therapy helps individuals identify and change negative thought patterns and behaviors that contribute to substance abuse.
- **Nutritional counseling**: A healthy diet can impact overall well-being, and nutritional counseling can provide seniors with guidance on making nutritious food choices.

Frequently Asked Questions

What Are Some Common Risk Factors for Senior Substance Abuse?

Some common risk factors for senior substance abuse include

chronic pain, loneliness, loss of loved ones, retirement, and limited social support. These factors can contribute to increased vulnerability and the use of substances as a coping mechanism.

How Does Social Isolation Contribute to Substance Abuse in Seniors?

Social isolation can contribute to substance abuse in seniors by increasing feelings of loneliness, depression, and anxiety, which may lead individuals to use substances as a coping mechanism. Lack of social support and meaningful connections can exacerbate this issue.

Are There Any Specific Health Conditions That Commonly Co-Occur with Substance Abuse in Seniors?

Yes, there are several health conditions that commonly co-occur with substance abuse in seniors. These include cardiovascular disease, liver disease, respiratory disorders, mental health disorders, and cognitive impairment, among others.

What Are Some Challenges in Diagnosing and Treating Co-Occurring Health Issues in Seniors with Substance Abuse?

Diagnosing and treating co-occurring health issues in seniors with substance abuse can be challenging due to factors such as multiple chronic conditions, cognitive impairment, and limited access to healthcare services.

Are There Any Specific Evidence-Based Interventions or Treatment Approaches That Have Shown Success in Helping Seniors with Co-Occurring Health Issues and Substance Abuse?

Evidence-based interventions and treatment approaches have shown success in addressing co-occurring health issues in seniors with substance abuse. These approaches include integrated care models, cognitive-behavioral therapy, medication-assisted treatment, and peer support programs.

Conclusion

In conclusion, addressing co-occurring health issues for seniors with substance abuse is crucial in ensuring their overall well-being.

The growing prevalence of senior substance abuse highlights the need for effective interventions that target both physical and mental health challenges. Substance abuse can have a detrimental impact on physical health, while also exacerbating mental health conditions.

By addressing these co-occurring issues, professionals can support seniors in their recovery process and improve their quality of life.

CHAPTER 7: RELAPSE PREVENTION STRATEGIES

In Chapter 7, we plunge into the crucial topic of relapse prevention strategies specifically designed for seniors struggling with substance abuse.

As we explore the unique challenges faced by this demographic, it becomes clear that a comprehensive understanding of their needs is essential for effective treatment.

By identifying triggers and high-risk situations, building a staunch support system, developing coping mechanisms and stress management techniques, and creating a healthy and structured daily routine, we can offer seniors the tools they need to maintain their sobriety and achieve lasting recovery.

But how do we navigate these strategies in a way that truly addresses the complexities of addiction in the senior population?

Join us as we uncover the answers and shed light on this important aspect of addiction treatment for seniors.

Key Takeaways
- Seniors face unique challenges when it comes to substance abuse, including aging-related vulnerabilities, physical health decline, social isolation, and cognitive changes.
- Physical health implications for seniors with

medication interactions can exacerbate the risks associated with substance use.
- **Social isolation**: Seniors may experience increased social isolation due to a range of factors such as retirement, loss of loved ones, or limited mobility. This isolation can contribute to feelings of loneliness and depression, which may trigger or perpetuate substance abuse.
- **Cognitive changes**: Aging can bring about cognitive changes, making it more difficult for seniors to remember medication schedules, attend therapy sessions, or engage in relapse prevention strategies. These cognitive impairments can hinder their recovery efforts.

Physical Health Implications

Understanding the unique challenges that seniors face in relation to their physical health is essential in providing effective support and guidance for their recovery from substance abuse.

As individuals age, their bodies undergo various changes that can impact their overall well-being. Seniors may experience a decline in physical strength, reduced organ function, and an increased susceptibility to illnesses and injuries. These physical health implications can have a significant impact on their ability to recover from substance abuse and maintain sobriety.

It is crucial for healthcare professionals and caregivers to be aware of these challenges and develop tailored strategies to address them. This may include regular health check-ups, medication management, and promoting physical activity and nutrition.

Social Isolation Factors

Social isolation can pose significant challenges for seniors in their recovery from substance abuse. As they age, many older

substance abuse include a decline in physical strength, reduced organ function, increased susceptibility to illnesses and injuries, and a potential impact on recovery.
- Social isolation factors such as limited social support, stigma and shame, and lack of transportation can contribute to mental health issues and overall well-being for seniors with substance abuse.
- Effective relapse prevention strategies for seniors include trigger recognition techniques, self-reflection, mindfulness practices, developing a support system, avoiding high-risk environments, and building coping mechanisms and stress management techniques.

Understanding the Unique Challenges for Seniors

As we explore the unique challenges that seniors face in managing substance abuse, it is important to approach the topic with empathy and understanding.

Aging-related vulnerabilities, such as physical health implications and social isolation factors, can significantly impact a senior's ability to overcome addiction.

Aging-Related Vulnerabilities

Seniors facing substance abuse encounter a unique set of challenges that are related to the process of aging. These aging-related vulnerabilities can further complicate their recovery journey. It is crucial for us to understand these challenges to provide the necessary support and guidance to seniors struggling with substance abuse.

Here are three key aging-related vulnerabilities to consider:
- **Physical health decline**: As seniors age, their physical health may deteriorate, making them more susceptible to the negative effects of substance abuse. Chronic pain, diminished organ function, and

adults may experience a decrease in social connections, leading to feelings of loneliness and isolation. This can have a profound impact on their mental health and overall well-being, making it even more difficult for them to sustain their recovery efforts.

To better understand the unique challenges faced by seniors in relation to social isolation, it is important to consider the following factors:

1. **Limited social support**: Seniors may have a smaller social network due to factors such as retirement, the loss of loved ones, or physical limitations, making it harder to rely on others for support.
2. **Stigma and shame**: Older adults may feel embarrassed or ashamed about their substance abuse, which can prevent them from seeking help and engaging in social activities.
3. **Lack of transportation**: Limited mobility and access to transportation can restrict seniors' ability to maintain social connections and participate in recovery support groups or therapy sessions.

Recognizing and addressing these social isolation factors is crucial in developing effective relapse prevention strategies for seniors. By providing support, fostering a sense of belonging, and promoting social engagement, we can help seniors overcome these challenges and maintain their recovery journey.

Identifying Triggers and High-Risk Situations

As seniors navigate their recovery journey, it is essential to equip them with the tools to identify triggers and high-risk situations.

Trigger recognition techniques can help individuals become more self-aware of the situations, emotions, or people that may lead to relapse.

Trigger Recognition Techniques

Seniors with substance abuse can benefit from developing effective techniques to recognize triggers and identify high-risk situations. By being able to identify triggers, seniors can gain a better understanding of the situations, emotions, or thoughts that may lead to substance abuse relapse.

Here are three trigger recognition techniques that can aid in relapse prevention:

1. **Self-reflection**: Encouraging seniors to reflect on their past experiences and identify patterns can help them recognize triggers. This involves exploring the circumstances surrounding previous relapses and identifying commonalities.
2. **Mindfulness practices**: Teaching seniors mindfulness techniques can help them become more aware of their thoughts, emotions, and bodily sensations. By being present in the moment, they can notice trigger cues and respond in a healthier way.
3. **Developing a support system**: Seniors should be encouraged to surround themselves with individuals who understand their struggles and can provide emotional support. A dedicated support system can be instrumental in recognizing triggers and providing assistance during high-risk situations.

High-Risk Environment Avoidance

To continue building upon their trigger recognition techniques, seniors with substance abuse can further enhance their relapse prevention strategies by focusing on high-risk environment avoidance and identifying potential triggers and situations that may increase their risk of relapse.

High-risk environments refer to places, people, or circumstances that are associated with substance use. Identifying and avoiding these environments is crucial for maintaining sobriety. For instance, if attending social gatherings where alcohol or drugs are present has been a trigger in the past, it may be helpful to find alternative social activities or support groups that do not involve substance use.

Additionally, individuals should be mindful of the people they surround themselves with, as negative influences can significantly impact their recovery journey.

Coping Strategies Utilization

Identifying triggers and high-risk situations is a crucial aspect of developing effective coping strategies for seniors with substance abuse. By understanding the specific situations, emotions, or people that can potentially lead to relapse, seniors can better prepare themselves to navigate these challenges and maintain their sobriety.

Here are three key points to consider when identifying triggers and high-risk situations:

1. **Self-reflection**: Encourage seniors to take the time to reflect on their past experiences and identify patterns or common factors that have led to relapse in the past. This self-awareness can help them recognize potential triggers in the future.
2. **External influences**: It is important to acknowledge that certain environments, such as being in the presence of old friends who still engage in substance abuse or frequenting places associated with drug or alcohol use, can increase the risk of relapse. Seniors should be encouraged to avoid such environments and seek out healthier alternatives.
3. **Emotional triggers**: Emotions like stress, loneliness, or boredom can also function as triggers for substance use. Encourage seniors to develop healthy coping mechanisms, such as engaging in hobbies, practicing relaxation techniques, or seeking support from friends and family, to manage these emotions effectively.

Building a Strong Support System

Building a strong support system is essential for seniors with substance abuse issues in their journey towards recovery.

Family involvement can provide a stable and loving environment, offering encouragement, and understanding.

Peer support groups can offer a sense of belonging and the opportunity to connect with others who have experienced similar challenges.

Additionally, professional counseling options can provide guidance, tools, and strategies to address underlying issues and develop coping mechanisms.

Family Involvement

Encouraging active participation from family members in the recovery process is crucial for seniors with substance abuse, as it helps build a strong support system that promotes long-term sobriety. Family involvement plays a vital role in the journey towards recovery, providing emotional support, encouragement, and accountability.

Here are three key reasons why family involvement is essential:

1. **Emotional Support**: Seniors struggling with substance abuse often experience feelings of loneliness and isolation. Family involvement helps create a safe and supportive environment where they can express their emotions without judgment.
2. **Encouragement and Motivation**: Family members can serve as a source of encouragement and motivation throughout the recovery process. Their unwavering support can inspire seniors to stay committed and motivated towards achieving sobriety.
3. **Accountability**: By involving family members in the recovery process, seniors are held accountable for their actions. Family members can provide guidance, monitor progress, and help prevent relapse by recognizing warning signs and intervening when

necessary.

Peer Support Groups

To enhance the support system for seniors with substance abuse, it is important to explore the benefits of connecting with peer support groups.

Peer support groups provide a safe and understanding environment where seniors can share their experiences, receive emotional support, and gain insights from others who have faced similar challenges. These groups offer a unique opportunity for seniors to connect with individuals who can relate to their struggles and provide a sense of belonging.

Being part of a peer support group can help seniors feel less isolated and alone in their journey towards recovery. Moreover, these groups offer valuable resources and information, as members often share strategies and coping mechanisms that have worked for them.

Professional Counseling Options

Professional counseling options play a crucial role in establishing a robust support system for seniors with substance abuse.

Seeking professional help can provide seniors with the guidance, tools, and resources necessary to overcome their addiction and maintain long-term recovery.

Here are three important benefits of professional counseling for seniors:

1. **Individualized Treatment**: Professional counselors work closely with seniors to develop personalized treatment plans that address their unique needs and challenges. This individualized approach allows seniors to receive the specific support they require to overcome their substance abuse.
2. **Emotional Support**: Counselors provide a safe

and non-judgmental space for seniors to express their emotions, fears, and frustrations. Through compassionate listening and empathy, counselors help seniors understand and manage their emotions in a healthy way, reducing the risk of relapse.

3. **Skill Building**: Professional counseling equips seniors with valuable coping skills and strategies to prevent relapse. Counselors teach seniors effective ways to manage triggers, manage stress, and make healthier choices, empowering them to maintain sobriety and live fulfilling lives.

Developing Coping Mechanisms and Stress Management Techniques

When it comes to relapse prevention, developing coping mechanisms and stress management techniques is crucial for seniors with substance abuse.

One effective technique is practicing breathing exercises for stress relief, which can help seniors calm their minds and bodies in challenging situations.

Additionally, adopting healthy coping strategies, such as engaging in hobbies or connecting with loved ones, can provide seniors with healthier alternatives to manage stress.

Breathing Exercises for Stress

To effectively manage stress and develop coping mechanisms, seniors with substance abuse can benefit from incorporating breathing exercises into their daily routine. Breathing exercises are a simple yet powerful tool that can help seniors calm their minds, reduce anxiety, and promote relaxation.

Here are three types of breathing exercises that can be particularly helpful for seniors:

- **Diaphragmatic breathing**: This technique involves breathing deeply into the diaphragm, rather than

shallowly into the chest. It helps seniors relax and slow down their breathing, which in turn reduces stress and promotes a sense of calm.
- **Box breathing**: This technique involves inhaling, holding the breath, exhaling, and holding again, each for an equal count of seconds. It can be done anywhere and anytime, providing seniors with a quick and effective way to manage stress.
- **Progressive muscle relaxation**: This technique involves systematically tensing and then releasing different muscle groups while focusing on deep breathing. It helps seniors achieve a state of deep relaxation and reduces muscle tension.

Healthy Coping Strategies

Developing healthy coping strategies and stress management techniques is crucial for seniors with substance abuse to effectively navigate their recovery journey. Substance abuse can be both physically and emotionally challenging, and having effective coping mechanisms is essential for maintaining sobriety and preventing relapse.

One important coping strategy is to identify and avoid triggers that may lead to substance abuse. This can involve avoiding certain people, places, or situations that may tempt individuals to use substances.

Additionally, engaging in activities that promote relaxation and self-care, such as exercise, meditation, or hobbies, can help seniors manage stress and reduce the urge to turn to substances.

It is also beneficial for seniors to build a support network of friends, family, and professionals who can provide guidance and encouragement throughout their recovery journey. Seeking therapy or counseling can also be immensely helpful in developing healthy coping strategies and addressing underlying emotional issues that may contribute to substance abuse.

Mindfulness for Stress Relief

Mindfulness techniques can be effective in helping seniors develop coping mechanisms and manage stress for relapse prevention in their substance abuse recovery journey. When practiced regularly, mindfulness can offer countless benefits, including:

- **Increased self-awareness**: Mindfulness allows seniors to become more attuned to their thoughts, emotions, and bodily sensations, helping them identify triggers and potential relapse warning signs.
- **Stress reduction**: By focusing on the present moment without judgment, seniors can learn to let go of worries about the past or future, promoting a sense of calm and reducing stress levels.
- **Emotional regulation**: Mindfulness practice can enhance seniors' ability to regulate their emotions, preventing them from turning to substances to cope with difficult feelings.
- **Improved impulse control**: Through mindfulness, seniors can cultivate a non-reactive and non-judgmental attitude, giving them the space to pause and make healthier choices instead of giving in to cravings.

Creating a Healthy and Structured Daily Routine

Establishing a healthy and structured daily routine is crucial for seniors with substance abuse issues to maintain their sobriety.

By setting consistent habits, such as waking up and going to bed at the same time each day, seniors can create a sense of stability and structure in their lives.

Additionally, setting realistic goals and implementing self-care practices, such as exercise and healthy eating, can help seniors maintain their overall well-being and prevent relapse.

Establishing Consistent Habits

Creating a healthy and structured daily routine is essential for seniors with substance abuse to maintain their sobriety and overall well-being. Establishing consistent habits can help seniors develop a sense of stability and purpose, reducing the risk of relapse.

Here are three key benefits of creating a structured daily routine:

1. **Stability**: Having a consistent routine provides a stable foundation for seniors in recovery. It helps them establish a sense of predictability and control over their lives, reducing feelings of anxiety and uncertainty.
2. **Time management**: A structured routine allows seniors to allocate their time wisely, ensuring they have a healthy balance between work, leisure activities, and self-care. This helps prevent boredom and idle time, which can be triggers for relapse.
3. **Accountability**: By following a daily routine, seniors can hold themselves accountable for their actions and choices. It provides a framework for making healthier decisions and avoiding situations that may jeopardize their sobriety.

Setting Realistic Goals

To further enhance their progress in maintaining sobriety and overall well-being, seniors with substance abuse can benefit from setting realistic goals as part of creating a healthy and structured daily routine.

Setting realistic goals allows seniors to have a clear direction and purpose, providing them with a sense of accomplishment and motivation. These goals should be specific, measurable, achievable, relevant, and time-bound (SMART).

By breaking down larger goals into smaller, manageable steps, seniors can avoid feeling overwhelmed and increase their chances of success.

It is important to remember that everyone's goals will be unique, taking into account their personal circumstances, interests, and abilities.

Implementing Self-Care Practices

Seniors with substance abuse can benefit from incorporating self-care practices into their daily routine to promote a healthy and structured lifestyle. Taking care of oneself is crucial in maintaining sobriety and preventing relapse. Here are three key self-care practices that can help seniors on their journey towards recovery:

- **Establishing a consistent sleep schedule**: Getting enough rest is essential for physical and mental wellbeing. Creating a regular sleep routine can improve sleep quality and provide seniors with the energy they need to navigate their day.
- **Engaging in regular physical activity**: Exercise not only improves physical health but also boosts mood and reduces stress. Seniors can try activities like walking, swimming, or yoga to stay active and maintain their overall wellbeing.
- **Practicing mindfulness and relaxation techniques**: Seniors can benefit from incorporating mindfulness and relaxation exercises into their daily routine. This can include meditation, deep breathing exercises, or engaging in activities that bring them joy and relaxation.

Frequently Asked Questions

What Are Some Common Misconceptions About Substance Abuse Among Seniors?

Common misconceptions about substance abuse among seniors include the belief that it is a normal part of aging, that older adults cannot become addicted, and that treatment is not effective. These misconceptions hinder proper understanding and support for this vulnerable population.

How Does Age-Related Physical Health Issues Contribute to Substance Abuse in Seniors?

Age-related physical health issues can contribute to substance abuse in seniors by increasing the likelihood of chronic pain, sleep disturbances, and mental health disorders. These challenges may lead to self-medication and the misuse of substances as a coping mechanism.

What Are Some Effective Ways to Address the Stigma Associated with Substance Abuse in Older Adults?

Addressing the stigma associated with substance abuse in older adults requires a comprehensive approach. Education about addiction, dispelling myths, promoting empathy, and providing support services can help reduce stigma and encourage individuals to seek help without judgment.

Are There Any Specific Warning Signs That Loved Ones Should Look Out for in Seniors Who May Be Struggling with Substance Abuse?

Loved ones should be aware of warning signs in seniors struggling with substance abuse, such as changes in behavior, mood swings, neglecting personal hygiene, and social withdrawal. Early recognition and intervention are crucial for successful relapse prevention and recovery.

How Can Healthcare Professionals Effectively Screen for Substance Abuse in Older Adults?

Healthcare professionals can effectively screen for substance abuse in older adults through comprehensive assessments that include physical exams, medical history reviews, and validated screening tools. Open and non-judgmental communication is crucial in establishing trust and identifying potential substance abuse issues.

Conclusion

In conclusion, it is crucial to recognize the unique challenges faced by seniors with substance abuse and provide them with effective relapse prevention strategies.

By understanding their triggers and high-risk situations, building a strong support system, developing coping mechanisms, and creating a healthy daily routine, seniors can improve their chances of maintaining sobriety.

Empathy, knowledge, and support are essential in helping seniors overcome substance abuse and live a fulfilling life in their golden years.

CHAPTER 8: REBUILDING RELATIONSHIPS AND COMMUNITY TIES

In Chapter 8, we explore the crucial process of rebuilding relationships and community ties for seniors with substance abuse issues.

Substance abuse not only takes a toll on an individual's physical and mental health, but it can also strain relationships and isolate seniors from their communities.

Understanding the impact of substance abuse on relationships is essential to address the barriers that may hinder the rebuilding process.

By identifying these barriers and implementing strategies to rebuild trust with loved ones, seniors can begin to reconnect with supportive community resources, fostering an environment that promotes healing and maintaining healthy relationships in recovery.

The journey towards rebuilding relationships and community ties is a complex and multifaceted one, and this chapter aims to shed light on the various aspects involved in this process, providing seniors with guidance and support as they navigate their path towards a fulfilling and connected life.

Key Takeaways

- Substance abuse strains relationships and causes damage that is difficult to repair, especially for seniors.
- Rebuilding trust and repairing family dynamics are crucial steps in restoring relationships and fostering a supportive community.
- Seniors face challenges in rebuilding relationships due to feelings of mistrust, fear, and isolation, and lack of support networks can hinder their efforts.
- Overcoming barriers to rebuilding community ties, such as social isolation and stigma, requires a compassionate and supportive approach from the community.

Understanding the Impact of Substance Abuse on Relationships

Substance abuse can have a profound impact on relationships, causing strain and damage that can be difficult to repair.

Loved ones may experience feelings of betrayal, anger, and mistrust, leading to breakdowns in communication and a loss of intimacy.

Rebuilding trust and repairing family dynamics are crucial steps in restoring relationships and fostering a supportive community for seniors struggling with substance abuse.

Relationship Strain After Abuse

The strain on relationships experienced by seniors after experiencing abuse can have a profound impact on their overall well-being and sense of community.

It is important to recognize that seniors who have gone through abuse, particularly related to substance abuse, often face immense challenges in rebuilding their relationships.

The damage caused by abuse can lead to feelings of mistrust, fear, and even isolation. These seniors may struggle to reconnect with loved ones and rebuild the trust that was lost.

It is crucial for their overall well-being and recovery that they receive support and understanding from their community.

Rebuilding Trust and Communication

After experiencing abuse, seniors often face significant challenges in rebuilding their relationships, especially when it comes to rebuilding trust and communication in the aftermath of substance abuse. Substance abuse can have a profound impact on relationships, eroding trust and creating barriers to effective communication.

Rebuilding trust is a delicate process that requires patience, understanding, and consistent effort. It is important for seniors to acknowledge the pain and damage caused by their substance abuse and take responsibility for their actions.

Effective communication is also crucial in rebuilding relationships. Seniors must learn to express themselves honestly and openly, while also actively listening to their loved ones' concerns and needs.

Seeking professional help, such as therapy or support groups, can provide valuable guidance and assistance in navigating these challenges.

Rebuilding trust and communication takes time, but with dedication and support, seniors can rebuild and strengthen their relationships.

Repairing Family Dynamics

Rebuilding family dynamics after substance abuse requires a deep understanding of the profound impact it has on relationships. Substance abuse can strain family bonds, erode trust, and create a sense of chaos within the household. To repair these dynamics, it is essential to approach the situation with empathy, knowledge, and support.

Here are three key steps to consider:

1. **Education and Awareness**: Family members need to understand the nature of substance abuse and its effects on both the individual and the family. By educating themselves about addiction, they can develop empathy and recognize that substance abuse is a disease rather than a moral failing.
2. **Open and Honest Communication**: Creating a safe space for open and honest communication is crucial. Encouraging family members to express their feelings, concerns, and expectations will facilitate healing and help rebuild trust.
3. **Establishing Boundaries**: Setting clear boundaries is important for both the individual in recovery and the family members. Establishing healthy boundaries will help restore a sense of stability and create an environment conducive to healing and growth.

Identifying Barriers to Rebuilding Community Ties

Rebuilding community ties for seniors with substance abuse can be a challenging process due to various barriers.

One of the main barriers is social isolation, as seniors may have withdrawn from their social networks during their substance abuse period.

Additionally, stigma and discrimination surrounding substance abuse can prevent seniors from reaching out for support and rebuilding relationships.

Lastly, the lack of support networks can hinder their efforts to reconnect with their community.

Understanding these barriers is crucial in developing effective strategies to help seniors overcome these challenges and rebuild their community ties.

Social Isolation Challenges

Social isolation presents significant challenges for seniors seeking to rebuild their community ties in the face of substance abuse. It is crucial to understand the barriers that contribute to this isolation and hinder the process of rebuilding relationships. Here are three familiar challenges that seniors face:

1. **Limited social networks**: Substance abuse can lead to strained relationships and a loss of social connections. Seniors may find themselves without a support system or people to turn to during their recovery journey.
2. **Stigma and shame**: The fear of judgment and stigma associated with substance abuse can cause seniors to withdraw from social activities and isolate themselves further. Overcoming this stigma is essential for rebuilding community ties.
3. **Physical and cognitive decline**: Aging can bring physical and cognitive challenges that may limit a senior's ability to engage in social activities. These limitations can contribute to feelings of isolation and make it difficult to reconnect with their community.

Addressing these challenges requires a compassionate and supportive approach that recognizes the unique needs of seniors facing substance abuse and encourages their reintegration into their communities.

Stigma and Discrimination

Addressing the challenges of stigma and discrimination is crucial in facilitating the process of rebuilding community ties for seniors facing substance abuse. Stigma and discrimination can have a detrimental impact on seniors, making it even more difficult for them to seek help and support.

It is important for us to understand that addiction is a complex issue that can affect anyone, regardless of age. Seniors facing substance abuse should not be judged or ostracized, but instead, they need our empathy and support.

Lack of Support Networks

As we continue our exploration of the challenges faced by seniors with substance abuse in rebuilding their community ties, it is important to acknowledge the significant barriers posed by the lack of support networks. When seniors do not have strong support systems in place, it can be incredibly difficult for them to overcome their substance abuse issues and reintegrate into their communities.

Here are three key reasons why the lack of support networks is a major obstacle for seniors in this situation:

1. **Isolation**: Seniors without support networks often feel isolated and alone, which can exacerbate their substance abuse problems. Without the presence of understanding friends or family members, they may struggle to find motivation and encouragement to seek help and recovery.
2. **Limited access to resources**: Support networks provide seniors with access to resources such as treatment centers, counseling services, and support groups. Without these resources, seniors may find it challenging to navigate the recovery process and access the help they need.
3. **Increased risk of relapse**: Support networks play a crucial role in preventing relapse by providing ongoing emotional support and accountability. Without these networks, seniors may be more vulnerable to relapse, as they may lack the necessary support to maintain their sobriety.

Recognizing the impact of the lack of support networks is crucial in developing effective strategies to rebuild relationships and community ties for seniors with substance abuse. By addressing this barrier, we can better support seniors on their journey to recovery and help them lead fulfilling lives within their communities once again.

Strategies for Rebuilding Trust with Loved Ones

Rebuilding trust with loved ones is a crucial step in the recovery process for seniors with substance abuse.

One effective strategy is to apologize and seek forgiveness for past actions, demonstrating a genuine willingness to change.

Open and honest communication is also essential, as it allows for the expression of emotions, concerns, and expectations.

Additionally, consistency and reliability in one's actions can help rebuild trust over time.

Apologizing and Seeking Forgiveness

When seeking to rebuild trust with loved ones after substance abuse, it is crucial to approach the process with sincerity, humility, and a genuine desire to make amends. Apologizing and seeking forgiveness can be challenging, but it is an essential step in rebuilding relationships. Here are three strategies to help you navigate this process:

1. **Take responsibility**: Acknowledge your actions and the impact they had on your loved ones. Accepting responsibility shows that you understand the hurt you caused and are committed to making changes.
2. **Express remorse**: Apologize sincerely and empathetically. Show that you understand the pain you caused and express genuine remorse for your actions. This can help your loved ones see your commitment to change and your desire to repair the relationship.
3. **Give them time and space**: Understand that rebuilding trust takes time. Your loved ones may need space to process their emotions and heal. Respect their boundaries and be patient, allowing them to decide when and how they are ready to forgive.

Open and Honest Communication

After apologizing and seeking forgiveness, the next crucial step in rebuilding trust with loved ones after substance abuse is through open and honest communication.

It is important to establish a safe and non-judgmental space where both parties feel comfortable expressing their thoughts and feelings.

This involves actively listening, being empathetic, and validating their emotions.

Transparency is key during these conversations, as it allows for a deeper understanding of the impact of substance abuse on both individuals.

It is essential to share personal experiences, fears, and concerns openly, while also being receptive to the concerns of loved ones.

Consistency and Reliability

Consistency and reliability play a crucial role in rebuilding trust with loved ones affected by senior substance abuse. When someone has struggled with substance abuse, their loved ones often feel betrayed and unsure of what to expect. Rebuilding trust requires consistent actions and reliable behavior over time.

Here are three strategies to help rebuild trust with your loved ones:

1. **Follow through on commitments**: It is important to show that you can be relied upon by following through on your promises. This means showing up when you say you will, completing tasks as agreed upon, and being consistent in your actions.
2. **Be honest and transparent**: Rebuilding trust requires open and honest communication. Share your progress, setbacks, and feelings with your loved ones. Being transparent about your journey will help them understand and support you better.

3. **Establish a routine**: Creating a routine can provide stability and predictability, which are key factors in rebuilding trust. Stick to a schedule, whether it is attending support group meetings, therapy sessions, or spending quality time with your loved ones.

Reconnecting With Supportive Community Resources

Reconnecting with supportive community resources is a crucial step in the journey of rebuilding relationships and community ties for seniors with substance abuse.

Community support groups provide a safe space to share experiences and receive encouragement from individuals facing similar challenges.

Local treatment centers offer specialized programs and resources to address substance abuse issues.

Reestablishing family connections can provide a strong support system for seniors on their path to recovery.

Community Support Groups

Community support groups provide a vital network for seniors struggling with substance abuse, offering a safe and understanding space to reconnect with supportive community resources. These groups serve as a lifeline for seniors seeking recovery by providing a sense of belonging, understanding, and encouragement.

Here are three key benefits of community support groups for seniors with substance abuse:

1. **Peer Support**: Community support groups offer the opportunity to connect with peers who have experienced similar challenges. Through sharing stories, listening, and empathizing, seniors can find comfort in knowing they are not alone in their journey towards recovery.

2. **Education and Resources**: These groups provide access to valuable information, resources, and referrals to specialized services. Seniors can learn about treatment options, coping strategies, and practical tips for maintaining sobriety.
3. **Emotional and Social Support**: Isolation is a common struggle for seniors with substance abuse issues. Community support groups offer a space to build new friendships, share experiences, and receive emotional support from individuals who understand the unique challenges faced by seniors.

Local Treatment Centers

Local treatment centers play a crucial role in facilitating the reconnection of seniors struggling with substance abuse to supportive community resources. These centers serve as a lifeline for seniors seeking help and support in their journey to recovery.

With their empathetic and knowledgeable staff, local treatment centers provide a safe and inclusive environment where seniors can receive the necessary care and guidance they need. These centers offer a range of services, including counseling, therapy, medication management, and support groups tailored specifically for seniors.

Reestablishing Family Connections

As seniors seek assistance and guidance in their journey towards recovery, one important aspect to address is the re-establishment of strong family connections and the utilization of supportive community resources.

Reconnecting with family members can provide a vital source of emotional support and understanding during this challenging time. It is crucial to rebuild trust and open lines of communication, fostering an environment of empathy and compassion.

Additionally, seniors should actively seek out supportive community resources that can provide guidance and assistance throughout their recovery process. These resources may include support groups, counseling services, or community centers that offer programs specifically tailored to the needs of seniors with substance abuse issues.

Maintaining Healthy Relationships in Recovery

Maintaining healthy relationships in recovery is crucial for seniors with substance abuse. Supportive social circles play a vital role in providing encouragement, understanding, and accountability.

Developing effective communication skills and setting boundaries can help seniors navigate their relationships and maintain their sobriety.

Supportive Social Circles

Developing and nurturing healthy relationships is a crucial aspect of recovery for seniors struggling with substance abuse. Supportive social circles can provide much-needed emotional support, encouragement, and accountability during the recovery process. Here are three key benefits of maintaining healthy relationships in recovery:

1. **Emotional support**: Having a supportive social circle can provide seniors in recovery with a safe space to express their feelings and emotions without judgment. This support can help them cope with the challenges they face during their journey towards sobriety.
2. **Encouragement and motivation**: Seniors in recovery often need encouragement and motivation to stay on track. Supportive relationships can provide the necessary inspiration and motivation to overcome obstacles and continue making progress.
3. **Accountability**: Healthy relationships can hold

seniors accountable for their actions and choices. Friends and loved ones who genuinely care about their well-being can help them stay committed to their recovery goals and avoid relapse.

Communication Skills

Effective communication skills are essential for maintaining healthy relationships in recovery for seniors struggling with substance abuse. The journey towards recovery can be challenging, and effective communication can play a crucial role in rebuilding relationships and community ties.

When seniors struggling with substance abuse learn how to communicate effectively, they can express their thoughts, feelings, and needs in a clear and respectful manner. This allows them to establish boundaries, set realistic expectations, and foster understanding with their loved ones.

Active listening is also a vital component of effective communication, as it demonstrates empathy and validates the experiences of others. By actively engaging in conversations and practicing effective communication skills, seniors can rebuild trust, repair broken relationships, and foster a supportive network that contributes to their overall recovery journey.

Setting Boundaries

As seniors struggling with substance abuse work towards rebuilding relationships and community ties, one crucial aspect they must address is setting boundaries to maintain healthy connections during their recovery journey.

Setting boundaries can be a challenging but necessary step in the recovery process. Here are three key reasons why setting boundaries is essential for seniors in substance abuse recovery:

1. **Self-care**: Setting boundaries allows seniors to prioritize their own well-being and recovery. By clearly defining their limits, they can protect themselves from potential triggers or situations that

may jeopardize their progress.
2. **Healthy relationships**: Boundaries help seniors establish healthy and respectful relationships with their loved ones. By communicating their needs and limitations, they can foster open and honest connections that support their recovery journey.
3. **Avoiding relapse**: Setting boundaries helps seniors create a structure that minimizes the risk of relapse. By setting limits on certain activities, environments, or individuals, they can reduce temptation and maintain their focus on sobriety.

Frequently Asked Questions

How Do Seniors with Substance Abuse Issues Rebuild Trust with Loved Ones?

Rebuilding trust with loved ones is crucial for seniors with substance abuse issues. It requires open communication, empathy, and a willingness to make amends. By demonstrating consistency, honesty, and a commitment to sobriety, seniors can gradually rebuild relationships and regain the trust of their loved ones.

What Are Some Common Barriers That Seniors Face When Trying to Rebuild Their Community Ties?

Seniors face common barriers when rebuilding community ties, such as stigma, lack of social support, and limited resources. These challenges can hinder their efforts to reconnect with their communities and regain a sense of belonging and purpose.

How Can Seniors Identify Community Resources That Can Support Their Recovery Journey?

Seniors can identify community resources to support their recovery journey by reaching out to local organizations, attending support groups, consulting with healthcare professionals, utilizing online directories, and engaging in social activities that promote connection and well-being.

What Strategies Can Seniors Use to Maintain Healthy Relationships While in Recovery?

Seniors in recovery can maintain healthy relationships by establishing clear boundaries, practicing open communication, and seeking support from their loved ones. It is crucial to prioritize self-care and engage in activities that promote overall well-being to sustain healthy relationships during the recovery process.

How Does Substance Abuse Impact Relationships and Community Ties for Seniors?

Substance abuse can have a profound impact on the relationships and community ties of seniors. It can lead to strained relationships, isolation, and withdrawal from social activities, causing a breakdown in support networks and a sense of disconnection from the community.

Conclusion

In conclusion, rebuilding relationships and community ties for seniors with substance abuse requires understanding the impact of substance abuse on relationships. It is crucial for seniors to reconnect with supportive community resources and maintain healthy relationships in recovery.

Identifying barriers to rebuilding community ties is another important aspect. Seniors may face challenges such as stigma, shame, and fear of judgment from their loved ones. These barriers need to be addressed and overcome for seniors to rebuild their community ties successfully.

Implementing strategies to rebuild trust with loved ones is also essential. Seniors need to communicate openly and honestly with their loved ones, demonstrate their commitment to recovery, and make amends for any past wrongs. These strategies can help rebuild trust and strengthen relationships.

By addressing these aspects, seniors can regain a sense of

belonging and support, leading to a more fulfilling and successful recovery journey.

CHAPTER 9: NAVIGATING LEGAL AND FINANCIAL CHALLENGES

Chapter 9 examines the complex and often overlooked legal and financial challenges faced by seniors struggling with substance abuse.

As the aging population continues to grow, it is crucial to address the unique needs of this vulnerable group. Understanding the legal implications, identifying available financial resources, advocating for legal rights, and overcoming financial barriers are just a few of the key topics explored in this chapter.

By navigating the intricate web of legal and financial support systems, seniors and their loved ones can find the necessary guidance and assistance to navigate this challenging landscape.

Discover the strategies, insights, and solutions that can help seniors with substance abuse overcome these obstacles and regain control of their lives.

Key Takeaways

- Substance abuse can lead to legal troubles, including DUIs and drug possession charges, for seniors.
- Seniors may face financial instability due to mounting debts, loss of employment, and legal

consequences.
- Seeking appropriate guidance and support, both legally and financially, is crucial for seniors and their loved ones.
- Identifying and accessing available financial resources, such as government assistance programs and insurance coverage, can help seniors with substance abuse issues.

Understanding the Legal Implications

Understanding the legal implications of substance abuse for seniors is crucial to navigate the potential legal consequences and financial challenges that may arise. Seniors who engage in substance abuse may face legal troubles such as DUIs or drug possession charges, which can lead to fines, probation, or even incarceration.

Additionally, substance abuse can significantly impact a senior's financial well-being, affecting their ability to manage their finances, plan for their future, or engage in estate planning.

It is important for seniors and their loved ones to be aware of these potential legal and financial hurdles and seek appropriate guidance and support.

Legal Consequences for Seniors

Seniors who are struggling with substance abuse face a multitude of legal challenges that can have significant implications for their well-being and overall quality of life. It is important to understand the legal consequences that seniors may encounter because of their substance abuse.

These consequences can include: - **Criminal charges**: Seniors may find themselves facing criminal charges related to drug possession, distribution, or driving under the influence. These charges can lead to fines, probation, or even imprisonment.

- **Family law issues**: Substance abuse can strain

familial relationships, leading to divorce or custody battles. Seniors may also face challenges in obtaining visitation rights or maintaining a relationship with their grandchildren.
- **Financial difficulties**: Substance abuse can lead to financial instability, as seniors may struggle to maintain employment or may face legal actions related to unpaid bills or debts.
- **Legal guardianship**: In some cases, seniors with substance abuse issues may require a legal guardian to make decisions on their behalf, further limiting their autonomy.

Navigating these legal consequences can be overwhelming for seniors. It is crucial for them to seek legal support and resources to understand their rights and options to protect their well-being and maintain their quality of life.

Financial Implications of Substance Abuse

The financial implications of substance abuse can have a significant impact on the lives of seniors. It creates a complex web of legal challenges and financial instability. For seniors struggling with substance abuse, their financial well-being can quickly deteriorate. They face mounting debts, loss of employment, and legal consequences. Substance abuse can lead to increased healthcare costs due to medical complications and the need for specialized treatment.

Seniors may also find themselves facing legal fees and fines resulting from criminal charges related to their substance abuse. Additionally, substance abuse can impair decision-making abilities. This leads seniors to make poor financial choices, such as spending savings on drugs or falling victim to financial scams.

It is crucial for seniors with substance abuse issues to seek support and resources to address their financial challenges. They need to regain stability in their lives.

Challenges With Estate Planning

Estate planning can present unique challenges for seniors struggling with substance abuse, as they navigate the legal implications surrounding the distribution of their assets and the protection of their loved ones' future. It is crucial for individuals in this situation to seek guidance from professionals who understand the complex intersection of addiction and estate planning.

Here are some of the challenges that seniors with substance abuse may face in their estate planning journey:

- **Ensuring the validity of the estate plan**: Substance abuse can impair decision-making abilities, raising concerns about the individual's capacity to create a legally binding estate plan.
- **Addressing potential disputes**: Substance abuse can strain familial relationships, leading to conflicts among beneficiaries and challenges to the estate plan's validity.
- **Protecting assets from misuse**: Individuals struggling with substance abuse may need to take measures to prevent their assets from being used to support their addiction.
- **Providing for dependents**: Seniors with substance abuse may have children or other dependents who require special consideration in the estate plan.

Navigating these challenges requires sensitivity and expertise to create a comprehensive estate plan that addresses the unique needs of seniors struggling with substance abuse. By seeking professional guidance, individuals can ensure that their assets are protected, their loved ones are provided for, and their wishes are upheld.

Identifying Financial Resources

When it comes to seniors struggling with substance abuse,

identifying financial resources is crucial in ensuring that they receive the necessary support and care.

Government assistance programs, such as Medicaid and Social Security, can provide financial aid for treatment services.

Additionally, exploring insurance coverage options and considering retirement savings can also help seniors access the financial resources they need to address their substance abuse challenges effectively.

Government Assistance Programs

Identifying financial resources through government assistance programs can provide crucial support for seniors facing legal and financial challenges due to substance abuse. These programs are designed to help and alleviate the financial burden that often accompanies such challenges.

Here are some key government assistance programs available for seniors:

- **Medicare**: This program provides healthcare coverage for individuals aged 65 and older, including coverage for substance abuse treatment and mental health services.
- **Supplemental Security Income (SSI)**: SSI provides financial assistance to low-income seniors with disabilities, including substance abuse disorders, to help cover basic needs such as food, shelter, and clothing.
- **Medicaid**: Medicaid offers healthcare coverage for low-income individuals, including seniors, and may cover substance abuse treatment services.
- **Social Security Disability Insurance (SSDI)**: SSDI provides financial assistance to seniors who are unable to work due to a disability, including substance abuse disorders.

These government assistance programs can provide seniors

with the financial resources they need to access essential healthcare services and support their recovery journey.

Insurance Coverage Options

Exploring the various insurance coverage options can be a critical step in identifying the financial resources available to seniors facing legal and financial challenges due to substance abuse. Insurance coverage can provide essential support for seniors seeking treatment, therapy, and other necessary services.

There are several types of insurance coverage options that seniors can consider, including Medicare, Medicaid, and private health insurance plans. Medicare is a federal health insurance program for individuals aged 65 and older, and it covers a range of services related to substance abuse treatment.

Medicaid, on the other hand, is a joint federal and state program that provides health coverage to low-income individuals, including seniors. Private health insurance plans can also offer coverage for substance abuse treatment, but the extent of coverage may vary depending on the specific plan.

It is important for seniors to carefully review and understand their insurance coverage options to ensure they are maximizing their benefits and accessing the necessary resources to address their substance abuse challenges.

Retirement Savings Considerations

As seniors navigate the challenges of substance abuse, it becomes imperative to consider retirement savings as a means of identifying the necessary financial resources for their recovery journey. Retirement savings can serve as a safety net, providing individuals with the means to access treatment, therapy, and support services.

Here are some considerations regarding retirement savings for seniors with substance abuse:

- **Assessing the available funds:** Evaluate the current retirement savings and determine if any portion can be allocated towards the recovery process.
- **Consulting financial advisors:** Seek guidance from professionals who can help navigate the complexities of retirement savings, ensuring that the necessary funds are used wisely.
- **Exploring withdrawal options:** Understand the potential penalties and tax implications associated with early withdrawal from retirement accounts.
- **Exploring alternative sources:** Consider other potential sources of financial support, such as loans, grants, or assistance programs.

Advocating for Legal Rights

Advocating for legal rights is crucial for seniors with substance abuse issues. They may face various legal challenges, but there are options available to ensure their rights are protected.

These include seeking legal representation, accessing healthcare services, and making informed financial decisions. By understanding and utilizing these resources, seniors can navigate the legal system with support and advocate for their rights effectively.

Legal Representation Options

Seniors facing substance abuse often encounter complex legal challenges, necessitating the need for effective legal representation to safeguard their rights and navigate the legal system. When it comes to advocating for legal rights, seniors have several options for obtaining the necessary legal representation. These options include:

- **Private Attorneys:** Hiring a private attorney gives seniors access to personalized legal assistance. Private attorneys can provide tailored guidance and representation based on the specific needs and

circumstances of each individual case.
- **Legal Aid Organizations**: Seniors with limited financial resources can seek assistance from legal aid organizations. These organizations offer free or low-cost legal services to individuals who meet certain income criteria. They can help seniors navigate legal processes and provide advice on their rights and options.
- **Public Defenders**: For seniors facing criminal charges related to substance abuse, public defenders can be appointed by the court if they are unable to afford a private attorney. Public defenders are experienced in handling criminal cases and can provide legal representation in court.
- **Pro Bono Services**: Some attorneys offer pro bono services, which means they provide legal representation for free. Seniors can explore pro bono options through local bar associations or legal aid organizations.

Access to Healthcare

Access to healthcare is a crucial aspect of advocating for the legal rights of seniors facing substance abuse. When it comes to addressing the healthcare needs of this vulnerable population, compassion, knowledge, and experience are paramount.

Seniors struggling with substance abuse require specialized medical attention that understands the complexities of their situation. Access to healthcare for these individuals involves ensuring they have access to comprehensive medical services that address both their physical and mental health needs. This includes providing screenings, assessments, and treatment options specifically tailored to seniors with substance abuse issues.

Additionally, healthcare access should encompass a multi-disciplinary approach, involving collaboration between healthcare providers, social workers, and legal professionals to create a holistic support system.

Financial Decision-Making

To effectively support seniors facing substance abuse, it is essential to address the complex issue of financial decision-making and advocate for their legal rights. Seniors with substance abuse problems may face unique challenges when it comes to managing their finances.

Here are some important considerations:

- **Impaired judgment**: Substance abuse can impair a senior's ability to make sound financial decisions, leading to financial instability and vulnerability.
- **Exploitation**: Seniors struggling with substance abuse may be more susceptible to financial exploitation by others who take advantage of their impaired state.
- **Legal protection**: Advocating for legal rights is crucial to ensure that seniors with substance abuse issues are protected from financial abuse and exploitation.
- **Support systems**: Seniors in need of financial decision-making assistance should have access to support systems such as legal representation, financial advisors, and caregivers who can help manage their finances responsibly.

Overcoming Financial Barriers

Overcoming financial barriers is a crucial aspect of helping seniors with substance abuse issues access the necessary treatment and support.

Budgeting for treatment costs is often a challenge, but it is important to explore available financial assistance options, such as grants or scholarships, which can help alleviate the burden.

Additionally, understanding insurance coverage and navigating the complexities of reimbursement can play a significant role in ensuring seniors receive the care they need without incurring overwhelming financial strain.

Budgeting for Treatment Costs

Navigating the financial obstacles associated with substance abuse treatment can be a daunting task for seniors, requiring careful budgeting and strategic planning. When it comes to budgeting for treatment costs, it is important to consider the following:

- **Treatment options**: Research different treatment options and their associated costs, such as inpatient rehab, outpatient programs, therapy sessions, and medication. This will help you understand the range of expenses you may encounter.
- **Insurance coverage**: Review your insurance policy to determine what substance abuse treatment services are covered. Familiarize yourself with any limitations, copayments, or deductibles that may apply.
- **Financial assistance**: Seek out potential sources of financial assistance, such as government programs, grants, or scholarships specifically designed to help seniors with substance abuse treatment costs.
- **Community resources**: Explore community resources that offer low-cost or free treatment options. Non-profit organizations, support groups, and local clinics may provide valuable assistance.

Accessing Financial Assistance

Seniors facing substance abuse challenges often encounter financial barriers that can impede their access to necessary treatment and support. It is crucial for these individuals to understand that there are options available to help overcome these financial hurdles.

One such option is accessing financial assistance programs specifically designed for seniors struggling with substance abuse. These programs can provide financial aid for treatment costs, including inpatient rehab, outpatient counseling, medications, and support services. Medicaid, for example, is a federal and state-funded program that offers coverage for substance abuse treatment to eligible seniors.

Additionally, there are nonprofit organizations and charities that provide grants and scholarships to seniors in need. Seeking guidance from social workers, case managers, or substance abuse treatment facilities can help seniors navigate the process of accessing financial assistance and find the resources they need to embark on their recovery journey.

Exploring Insurance Coverage

Exploring options for insurance coverage is essential in addressing the financial barriers that seniors facing substance abuse may encounter. Insurance coverage can provide the necessary financial support for seniors to access the treatment and care they need.

Here are some important considerations when exploring insurance coverage:

- **Coverage Types**: Understanding the different types of insurance coverage available, such as Medicare, Medicaid, or private insurance, can help seniors make informed decisions about their treatment options.
- **In-Network Providers**: Checking whether the insurance plan includes a network of providers who specialize in substance abuse treatment can ensure seniors receive comprehensive and specialized care.
- **Coverage Limits**: Being aware of coverage limits, such as the number of therapy sessions or medication coverage, can help seniors plan their treatment accordingly and avoid unexpected

expenses.

- **Pre-Authorization and Prior Approval**: Familiarizing oneself with the pre-authorization and prior approval processes can prevent delays in accessing treatment and ensure insurance coverage for necessary services.

Navigating Legal and Financial Support Systems

Navigating the legal and financial support systems can be daunting for seniors struggling with substance abuse. Understanding the legal documentation requirements, such as powers of attorney and healthcare proxies, is crucial for protecting their rights and making important decisions.

Additionally, exploring financial assistance options, such as Medicaid or Social Security benefits, can provide the necessary resources for treatment and support.

Social services can also play a vital role in connecting seniors with the appropriate legal and financial resources, ensuring they receive the assistance they need.

Legal Documentation Requirements

When addressing the legal and financial challenges faced by seniors with substance abuse, it is essential to understand the significance of meeting the necessary legal documentation requirements within the complex framework of legal and financial support systems. These requirements serve as the foundation for ensuring that seniors receive the appropriate assistance and protection they need.

Here are some key legal documentation requirements to consider:

- **Power of Attorney**: This document grants a trusted individual the authority to make legal and financial decisions on behalf of the senior.
- **Healthcare Directive**: This document outlines the senior's preferences and instructions regarding

medical treatment and end-of-life care.
- **Will or Trust**: These documents detail how the senior's assets and property will be distributed after their passing.
- **Guardianship/Conservatorship**: In cases where seniors are unable to make decisions for themselves, these legal arrangements appoint a responsible person to act on their behalf.

Financial Assistance Options

As seniors facing substance abuse contend with the legal and financial challenges before them, it becomes crucial to navigate the intricate landscape of legal and financial support systems, particularly when seeking financial assistance options.

For seniors struggling with substance abuse, financial assistance can be a lifeline in their journey towards recovery. There are various avenues available to seniors seeking financial support, including government programs, community resources, and private organizations.

Government programs such as Medicaid and Medicare can provide coverage for substance abuse treatment and related services. Additionally, seniors may be eligible for Social Security Disability Insurance (SSDI) or Supplemental Security Income (SSI) if their substance abuse has resulted in a disability.

Community resources, such as local charities, religious organizations, and non-profit foundations, also offer financial assistance options for seniors in need.

Lastly, private organizations may provide scholarships or grants specifically targeted towards seniors with substance abuse issues. Navigating these financial assistance options can be complex, but with the help of knowledgeable professionals and resources, seniors can find the support they need to overcome their challenges and embark on a path to recovery.

Support From Social Services

Obtaining support from social services is crucial for seniors facing substance abuse as they navigate the intricate landscape of legal and financial support systems. Social services can provide a lifeline for seniors by offering a range of assistance programs and resources.

Here are some ways social services can support seniors with substance abuse:

- **Case management**: Social workers can provide personalized support, helping seniors access the appropriate legal and financial services they need.
- **Counseling and therapy**: Seniors can benefit from individual or group therapy sessions, addressing the underlying causes of substance abuse and providing tools for recovery.
- **Support groups**: Joining support groups with peers who are facing similar challenges can offer a sense of community and solidarity.
- **Referrals to specialized programs**: Social services can connect seniors to specialized substance abuse treatment programs specifically designed for older adults.

With the help of social services, seniors can receive the support they need to navigate the legal and financial challenges associated with substance abuse.

Frequently Asked Questions

How Can Seniors with Substance Abuse Navigate the Legal Implications of Their Condition When It Comes to Employment?

Seniors with substance abuse face unique challenges when it comes to navigating the legal implications of their condition in relation to employment. Understanding the legal rights and protections available is crucial in ensuring fair treatment and support in the workplace.

Are There Any Specific Financial Resources Available for Seniors with Substance Abuse Who Are Unable to Work Due to Their Condition?

Seniors with substance abuse who are unable to work due to their condition may have access to specific financial resources. These resources can provide assistance with living expenses, medical costs, and rehabilitation programs to support their recovery and well-being.

What Steps Can Seniors with Substance Abuse Take to Advocate for Their Legal Rights in Terms of Housing and Accommodation?

Seniors with substance abuse can advocate for their legal rights in housing and accommodation by seeking assistance from legal professionals experienced in elder law and substance abuse. They can also research and access resources provided by local and national organizations specializing in housing rights for seniors.

How Can Seniors with Substance Abuse Overcome Financial Barriers When It Comes to Accessing Necessary Treatment and Rehabilitation Programs?

Seniors with substance abuse can overcome financial barriers to accessing necessary treatment and rehabilitation programs by exploring various options available, such as Medicare, Medicaid, private insurance, grants, and scholarships. Consulting with professionals and advocacy organizations can provide guidance and support.

What Support Systems Are Available to Help Seniors with Substance Abuse Navigate the Legal and Financial Aspects of Their Condition While Also Managing Their Overall Well-Being?

Several support systems are available to help seniors with substance abuse navigate the legal and financial aspects of their condition while also managing their overall well-being. These systems provide guidance, resources, and assistance to ensure seniors receive the necessary support and care they need.

Conclusion

In conclusion, navigating the legal and financial challenges for seniors with substance abuse requires a compassionate and knowledgeable approach.

Understanding the legal implications, identifying available financial resources, advocating for legal rights, and overcoming financial barriers are essential steps in providing support to this vulnerable population.

By navigating the complex legal and financial support systems, we can ensure that seniors receive the assistance they need to overcome substance abuse and maintain their well-being.

CONCLUSION:

As we conclude this book, it is important to reflect on the journey we have embarked upon.

Substance abuse among seniors is a complex issue that requires a multifaceted approach. Throughout this exploration, we have explored the power of supportive relationships, the vital role of friends, and the impact of family. We have also emphasized the importance of embracing self-care and wellness, prioritizing personal well-being, and cultivating healthy lifestyle habits.

Now, as we reach the final words of encouragement and inspiration, it is essential to celebrate the victories, big and small, that have been achieved along the way.

So, let us explore the milestones and achievements that have been attained, and recognize the progress that has been made thus far.

The Power of Supportive Relationships

Building and maintaining supportive relationships can play a vital role in the journey towards recovery from substance abuse for seniors. Friends and family members, who can offer understanding, love, and encouragement, have a significant impact on seniors' overall well-being and ability to overcome addiction.

These supportive relationships provide much-needed emotional support, reduce feelings of isolation, and serve as a source of motivation and strength.

Vital Role of Friends

Supportive relationships play a crucial role in the journey towards overcoming substance abuse, providing seniors with the strength, understanding, and encouragement they need to reclaim their lives.

Friends who offer unwavering support and empathy can make a significant difference in the recovery process. They can serve as a source of inspiration, reminding seniors of their worth and potential.

By being present and available, friends can provide a safe space for seniors to share their struggles, fears, and achievements. They can offer a listening ear, non-judgmental advice, and a shoulder to lean on.

Friends can also play an active role in helping seniors develop healthy coping mechanisms, engage in positive activities, and maintain sobriety.

The power of supportive relationships should not be underestimated, as they can be instrumental in providing seniors with the strength and motivation to overcome substance abuse and live fulfilling lives.

Family's Impact

The impact of family on seniors struggling with substance abuse cannot be overstated, as their support and understanding can be the foundation for successful recovery. Family plays a crucial role in the lives of seniors dealing with substance abuse issues, providing a source of love, care, and encouragement. When seniors have a dedicated support system in place, they are more likely to seek help and stay committed to their recovery journey.

Family members can offer empathy, knowledge, and support that are essential for seniors to overcome substance abuse. They can help seniors navigate the challenges of recovery, offering a listening ear, understanding, and guidance. By being present and involved, family members can provide the motivation and accountability needed to maintain sobriety.

Moreover, family involvement in treatment programs can significantly enhance the chances of successful recovery. Family therapy sessions can address underlying issues, improve communication, and rebuild trust and understanding. These sessions can also educate family members about addiction, enabling them to provide the necessary support and create a healthy environment for their loved ones.

Seniors struggling with substance abuse need the love, care, and understanding of their families. By offering a supportive and nurturing environment, families can empower their loved ones in their journey towards recovery.

Embracing Self-Care and Wellness

As seniors navigate the journey towards recovery from substance abuse, it is crucial for them to prioritize their personal well-being and embrace self-care and wellness.

This involves cultivating healthy lifestyle habits that promote physical, mental, and emotional well-being.

Prioritizing Personal Well-Being

To lead fulfilling and healthy lives, seniors must prioritize personal well-being by embracing self-care and wellness. Taking care of oneself becomes increasingly important as we age, and it is never too late to start focusing on our own well-being. Here are three essential elements to consider when prioritizing personal well-being:

1. **Physical Health**: Engage in regular exercise, eat a balanced diet, and get enough sleep. These practices can improve overall health, boost mood, and increase energy levels.
2. **Emotional Well-being**: Take time to connect with loved ones, engage in activities that bring joy, and practice stress management techniques such as deep breathing or meditation. Prioritizing emotional well-

being can enhance mental health and provide a sense of fulfillment.
3. **Mental Stimulation**: Engage in activities that challenge the mind, such as reading, puzzles, or learning a new skill. Keeping the mind active and curious can help maintain cognitive abilities and promote a sense of purpose.

Cultivating Healthy Lifestyle Habits

Prioritizing personal well-being lays the foundation for cultivating healthy lifestyle habits, allowing seniors to embrace self-care and wellness with a renewed sense of purpose and vitality.

As we age, it becomes increasingly important to take care of our physical, mental, and emotional health. Engaging in regular exercise, such as walking, yoga, or swimming, can improve strength, flexibility, and overall well-being. Eating a balanced diet that includes fruits, vegetables, whole grains, and lean proteins can provide the essential nutrients our bodies need.

Additionally, staying socially connected and maintaining meaningful relationships can have a positive impact on mental and emotional well-being. Taking time for oneself, engaging in hobbies or activities that bring joy, and practicing relaxation techniques like deep breathing or meditation can also contribute to a healthy lifestyle.

Celebrating Victories, Big and Small

As seniors on the road to recovery from substance abuse, it is important to celebrate every milestone and achievement, no matter how big or small.

Recognizing the progress made along this journey can be a powerful motivator and reminder of how far you have come.

Whether it is a day of sobriety, completing a treatment program, or achieving personal goals, each victory deserves to be acknowledged and celebrated.

Milestones and Achievements

Throughout your journey towards recovery, it is essential to acknowledge and celebrate the milestones and achievements, both big and small, that you have accomplished along the way. These milestones reflect your strength, resilience, and determination to overcome the challenges of addiction. Celebrating victories, no matter how small, can provide a sense of motivation and reinforce your progress.

Here are three significant milestones and achievements to honor:

1. **The decision to seek help**: Taking the first step towards recovery is a courageous act that deserves recognition. It shows your commitment to change and your willingness to face the difficulties ahead.
2. **Completing a treatment program**: Successfully completing a treatment program is a major milestone. It demonstrates your dedication to your recovery journey and your ability to learn new coping skills and strategies.
3. **Maintaining sobriety**: Each day, week, or month of sobriety is an accomplishment worth celebrating. It reflects your ongoing commitment to a healthier, substance-free life and highlights your growing resilience and self-discipline.

Recognizing Progress

Recognizing the progress made on the journey to recovery is an essential aspect of celebrating victories, both big and small, in overcoming substance abuse. It is important to acknowledge and honor the steps taken towards a healthier and happier life.

Recovery is not a linear process; it is filled with difficulties. By recognizing progress, we remind ourselves that every step forward counts, regardless of its size. Whether it is completing a month of sobriety, attending support group meetings regularly, or making positive changes in one's lifestyle, each achievement deserves recognition.

Celebrating these victories can boost self-confidence and motivation to continue the path of recovery. It is crucial to remember that progress is a personal journey, and comparing oneself to others can be counterproductive. Embrace your own milestones and achievements and let them inspire you to keep moving forward.

Frequently Asked Questions

How Can Seniors Find Supportive Relationships if They Are Currently Isolated or Have Strained Relationships with Family and Friends?

Seniors can find supportive relationships by reaching out to community organizations, attending support groups, or seeking professional counseling. Building new friendships based on common interests and joining social clubs can also help combat isolation and strengthen their support network.

What Are Some Self-Care Practices Specifically Beneficial for Seniors Recovering from Substance Abuse?

Seniors recovering from substance abuse can benefit from self-care practices tailored to their unique needs. These may include regular exercise, healthy eating, engaging in hobbies, seeking support from therapists or support groups, and practicing stress-reducing techniques such as meditation or mindfulness.

How Can Seniors Overcome Feelings of Guilt or Shame Associated with Their Past Substance Abuse and Focus on Celebrating Their Victories?

Seniors can overcome feelings of guilt or shame associated with past substance abuse by acknowledging and accepting their past, seeking support from others who understand, focusing on their progress and accomplishments, and engaging in self-care practices that promote healing and growth.

Are There Any Resources or Programs Specifically Designed to Support Seniors in Their Recovery Journey?

Yes, there are resources and programs specifically designed to support seniors in their recovery journey. These include support groups, counseling services, and rehabilitation centers that cater to the unique needs and challenges faced by older individuals dealing with substance abuse.

How Can Seniors Maintain Their Motivation and Continue Their Recovery Efforts in the Face of Setbacks or Challenges?

Seniors can maintain their motivation and continue their recovery efforts by staying connected with support networks, engaging in regular therapy or counseling, setting realistic goals, practicing self-care, and celebrating their progress. Challenges and setbacks can be overcome with determination, resilience, and a willingness to seek help when needed.

Conclusion

In conclusion, seniors facing substance abuse can find hope and strength in supportive relationships, self-care practices, and celebrating their victories.

By surrounding themselves with understanding and empathetic individuals, seniors can receive the necessary encouragement and guidance to overcome their struggles.

Embracing self-care and wellness will also play a crucial role in their recovery journey.

Remember, every step forward, no matter how small, is a victory worth celebrating.

Stay strong, believe in yourself, and never hesitate to seek help when needed.

BOOKS BY THIS AUTHOR

The 12-Steps Handbook: A Practical Guide To Recovery

ASIN : B0C9S8B486

Whether you are personally struggling with addiction, supporting a loved one in recovery, or seeking a deeper understanding of the 12-step process, "The 12-Steps Handbook" is an essential companion. It offers a wealth of knowledge, inspiration, and guidance to help individuals reclaim their lives, heal past wounds, and embrace a future filled with hope, resilience, and lasting recovery.

Beyond The 12 Steps: A Comprehensive Guide To Addiction And Recovery

ASIN : B0CQTP6M4N

In this illuminating guide, author John R. draws upon years of personal experience to offer a fresh perspective on addiction recovery. Moving beyond the limitations of the traditional 12-step model, this book explores a variety of evidence-based strategies and holistic approaches that address the root causes of addiction.

The 12-Steps Handbook (Pocket Size): A Practical Guide To Recovery

ASIN : B0CQY26X6L

This is a smaller, personal-sized version of "The 12-Steps Handbook: A Practical Guide to Recovery."

Whether you are personally struggling with addiction, supporting a loved one in recovery, or seeking a deeper understanding of the 12-step process, "The 12-Steps Handbook" is an essential companion. It offers a wealth of knowledge, inspiration, and guidance to help individuals reclaim their lives, heal past wounds, and embrace a future filled with hope, resilience, and lasting recovery.

Printed in Great Britain
by Amazon

40716751R00096